EUROPA ⚔ MILITARIA

THE SCOTTISH REGIMENTS

Ted Nevill

The Crowood Press

Dedication:
This book is dedicated to Erskine Hospital, which for 80 years has cared for Scotland's war veterans and ex-servicemen and women; its Erskine 2000 Appeal will allow this commitment to be carried forward into the 21st century, with a new 180-bed centre.

First published in 1999 by
The Crowood Press Ltd
Ramsbury, Marlborough, Wiltshire SN8 2HR

British Library Cataloguing-in-Publication Data
A catalogue record for this book is available from the British Library

ISBN 1 86126 284 1

Edited by Martin Windrow
Designed by Frank Ainscough/ Compendium
Printed and bound by Craft Print, Singapore

Acknowledgements:
This book is offered as a tribute to the Scottish Regiments and their soldiers, Regular and Territorial Army. Too brief to do them justice, it is a glimpse, taken over the past two years, into their life and traditions. Thanks is due to them for their help, patience and good humour when faced with yet more questions and a request for yet another photograph. The book would not have been possible without the co-operation of the Commanding Officers, Adjutants, and unit press officers of the eight Regular and six Territorial regiments featured; of the Directors of Music of the Lowland and Highland Bands; and of Lesley Edgar and Martine McNee of Media Ops at Army HQ Scotland. This assistance has been greatly appreciated.

Unless otherwise credited all the photographs have been taken by the author, whose thanks are offered to the units and photographers who have contributed. Particular gratitude must be expressed for the generous co-operation of Mark Owens, photographer at Army HQ Scotland, whose excellent pictures filled many gaps.

Finally, Martin Windrow deserves a mention for his patience, and for his hard work in converting crude scribblings into something intelligible.

Front cover:
Drum Major, 1st Bn., The King's Own Scottish Borderers, at Dreghorn Barracks, Edinburgh.
Back cover:
Two soldiers of 1st Bn., The Royal Scots during an exercise in Kenya.

Contents

Introduction

For the British Army the late 1960s were a dreary period of gradual disengagement from many overseas commitments. No major operations were being pursued; but troops were obliged to carry out a number of thankless missions as they withdrew from former strategic postings - sometimes under harassment from local armed groups, to which they were forbidden to respond "provocatively". The Wilson government had decided to abandon nearly all bases east of Suez, and to concentrate Britain's diminished capabilities in the NATO heartland facing the Iron Curtain.

This may have been unavoidable, given Britain's financial decline; but it was bad for service morale, and was quietly resented by that still considerable part of the British public which felt respect and affection for their forces. The Labour Party which then formed the government was traditionally unsympathetic towards, even suspicious of the armed services;

and the growing international hostility towards America's war in Vietnam contributed, by association, to a pervading anti-military atmosphere in the media.

One of the more fly-blown corners of empire from which Britain was then withdrawing was the Aden Protectorate, the region surrounding that strategic port in southern Arabia. Power was to be handed over to an independent Federation of South Arabia; but the FSA authorities were at best obstructive, and two distinct terrorist organisations - the NLF and FLOSY - were feuding for power in the imminent aftermath of British withdrawal. Restrictive orders limited the garrison's response to violence directed against both British soldiers and local civilians; and during 1967 alone the casualties totalled 240 local dead and 551 injured, and among British servicemen 44 dead and 325 injured. In June 1967 the 1st Battalion, The Argyll & Sutherland Highlanders arrived in the Protectorate under the command of Lt.Col.Colin Campbell Mitchell. Shortly afterwards a mutiny by local police in the central Crater district of Aden town left 22 dead and led to the withdrawal of the security forces without even recovering the bodies.

On 3 July 1967, led by the pipe major and to the stirring strains of 'Monymusk' - a tune which had preceded their attacks for generations - the Argylls briskly re-occupied the Crater district. Within two days Operation Stirling Castle (named after the home of the regiment) saw the Argylls, alongside the armoured cars of The Queen's Dragoon Guards, re-establish British control over the district. There were to be no casualties on the British side.

(Below) Aden, summer 1967: a foot patrol from 1st Bn., Argyll & Sutherland Highlanders is escorted by a Ferret scout car probably of The Queen's Dragoon Guards, who supported the Argylls' reoccupation of the Crater district in early July. They keep a wary eye open for possible attack by terrorists of the National Liberation Front or their rivals, the Front for the Liberation of Occupied South Yemen. As this was classed as an 'internal security' operation no battle honours were awarded to the units which served in Aden. (Soldier Magazine)

Back home the reports of this minor but unfashionably positive action captured the public imagination, reminding them of the well-established reputation of the Scottish regiments; the press made the Argylls' charismatic commanding officer a household name, and quickly dubbed him 'Mad Mitch'. In reality the operation was unwanted by Mitchell's superiors, who were concerned only with the trouble-free management of British retreat from Aden five months later; and their subsequent treatment of Lt.Col.Mitchell was mean-spirited.

To the British public, however, frustrated by the casualties and apparent futility of the post-colonial wars, there was something deeply satisfying in the sight of a Scottish regiment, pipes playing, taking on an enemy with panache and courage and - importantly - winning. When the Argylls were soon afterwards threatened with disbandment, a nationwide petition of protest gathered a million signatures.

* * *

The British Army is proud of its regimental system; and Scotland has given that army some of its finest regiments. Something within the Scottish character, responding to the turbulent history of their nation, has produced a people adept at warfare. A tradition of service passed down through generations, combined with loyalty, courage and fighting ability, has given the Scottish regiments an enviable reputation around the world.

The quality of Scottish fighting men was recognized as early as the 15th century, when King Charles VII of France maintained a Scottish bodyguard. Later Gustav Adolphus, the 17th century King of Sweden and one of military history's 'great captains', was to employ in the Thirty Years' War no less than thirteen Scottish mercenary regiments, one of them raised by John Hepburn in 1625. It was John Hepburn who in 1633 was authorized by King Charles I of England and Scotland to raise a further 1,200 recruits in Scotland for service in France, initially under the title *Le Régiment d'Hebron*. Returning to the service of the British Crown

A naif but typically spirited impression of battle in the 'high Victorian' style: the storming of the Heights of Alma in the Crimea, September 1854, by the 1st Division, comprising the Grenadier, Coldstream and Scots Fusilier Guards, the 42nd, 79th and 93rd Highlanders; the troops in the foreground are English Line infantry. (TRH Pictures)

in 1678, this unit would become The Royal Scots, and can thus claim precedence as Britain's senior Line infantry regiment - the 1st of Foot - by virtue of this 1633 warrant.

Over the years the history of the Scottish regiments has tracked that of the United Kingdom, the British Army and Empire, expanding or contracting in response to the needs of service to Crown and country. Wherever the Union Flag was hoisted across the world, the Scottish volunteer soldier played a disproportionate part in planting it and defending it. Scots put on the king's red jacket to fight in the major wars of the 18th century against the French, in Continental Europe and in the North American and Indian campaigns which layed the foundations of the British Empire.

During the twenty-year wars against Revolutionary and Napoleonic France the 42nd Black Watch and 26th Cameronians, the 71st Highland Light Infantry and 92nd Gordons, the Scots Greys of the 2nd 'Royal North British' Dragoons, and many shorter-lived regiments became famous for their unrivalled ésprit de corps, their prowess in battle and their good discipline on the march and in camp. While the tradition of the 'clan regiment' has been overstated, there is no doubt that the local recruiting of both officers and men of the Scottish regiments gave them more the character of families, keeping much closer links with their home communities, than the more mixed English regiments.

In the long Imperial years after Waterloo the Scottish regiments were to be found wherever the British Army was committed to extend or guard the frontiers of empire. In victory and defeat alike they added to their accumulation of battle honours. In the late Victorian period army re-organization saw the old numbered Regiments of Foot retitled after their recruiting areas, and many of the old Scottish traditional names became official; each now had two battalions, one usually serving in the UK and the other overseas. As the years passed the traditions and distinctions of dress evolved; and even today, after many amalgamations, the heritage of the old regiments can still be traced in the full dress of the new merged units.

When the call to arms sounded again in 1914 Scotland responded once more, contributing a disproportionate number of newly raised battalions for the old regiments, whether Regular, Territorial, or - from 1916 - conscript. Four complete divisions fought on the Western Front and at Gallipoli: the 9th and 15th (Scottish), 51st (Highland) and 52nd (Lowland) Divisions. In the Second World War the 15th, 51st and 52nd took the field once again; many other wartime-only units were raised, and Scottish infantry, tank crews, gunners, paratroopers, and soldiers of every other category fought everywhere from Dunkirk to Egypt, from Norway to Burma.

Victory in 1945 led to the rapid reduction of the Regular Army, and the Territorial Army returned to part-time service. By 1949 the 2nd Battalions of all the Scottish regiments except for The Scots Guards had been amalgamated or disbanded. A string of colonial campaigns, and the major clash of the Cold War in Korea in 1950-53, occupied the attention of the British Army and, as always, its Scottish regiments. But by 1958 another round of cuts had been decreed, and not even all the old 1st Battalions were safe.

January 1959 saw the merger of The Royal Scots Fusiliers with The Highland Light Infantry to form The Royal Highland Fusiliers. Two years later The Seaforth Highlanders and The Queen's Own Cameron Highlanders formed The Queen's Own Highlanders. Continuing withdrawals from overseas commitments led to further reductions between 1968 and 1970. In 1968 a meeting of the Council of Scottish Colonels decided that no more Scottish regiments should amalgamate: so one regiment was to disappear altogether, and The Cameronians (The Scottish Rifles) was chosen as the junior regiment within the Lowland Brigade. It had a unique history. The original 'Cameronians' were raised from the Scottish Presbyterian sect of Covenanters in 1689, and named after their leader Richard Cameron, who had been killed at Airds Moss in 1680. As the 26th (Cameronian) Regiment they merged in 1881 with the 90th (Perthshire) Light Infantry, itself raised in 1794. These religious origins led to unique customs, including the issue of a Bible to each recruit; the carrying of rifles and posting of sentries at their church services or 'Conventicles'- in commemoration of the secret religious gatherings which the armed Covenanters had been forced to hold out on the moors; and not taking the 'Loyal Toast'.

The Argyll & Sutherland Highlanders were luckier. The ably orchestrated public campaign to save a regiment which had recently cheered up so many British breakfast tables achieved some success; although reduced to a single company in 1971, it was restored to a full battalion a year later. The year 1968 earned its place in history; it was the first year since the Second World War during which no British soldier had died in action. It was a false dawn; the colonial wars may have ended, but an even uglier conflict was to break out much closer to home. In 1969 the British Army were to find themselves on the streets of Northern Ireland as

The last days of empire: a 'jock', probably of the 1st Argyll & Sutherland Highlanders, in the Suez Canal Zone, Egypt, December 1956. His dress and equipment are still typical of the Second World War: khaki serge battledress, pullover, a large khaki 'tam-o'-shanter' bonnet (TOS), 1937 webbing, and a .303 Rifle No.4 with an extra bandolier slung round the waist.

inter-communal unrest over civil rights broke out into serious rioting and violence. The 1st Bn., Royal Highland Fusiliers were the first Scottish unit posted to Ulster, and were in Londonderry in February 1970. The thirty years of unrest and terrorism which have followed have seen countless tours of duty by Scottish battalions in that unhappy province; and even with a 'peace process' ostensibly in place at the time of writing, Northern Ireland remains the British Army's largest operational commitment.

The recapture of the Falkland Islands from Argentine invasion in 1982, and the Gulf War in 1991, proved again - as if proof were needed - the professionalism of the British Army in two completely different combat scenarios; and Scottish soldiers again played their part. But the biggest postwar change in the structure of the British forces was soon to be prompted by an almost unimaginable event: the collapse of the Warsaw Pact and the end of the Cold War. However, with the removal of the Soviet Union's domination of politics in Eastern Europe, Yugoslavia soon broke up into warring states and communities, bringing an explosive and barbaric conflict to the doorstep of Western Europe. Freed from the threat from the Warsaw Pact, NATO has been able and willing to intervene, creating another overseas commitment for the British Army which could last for many years.

The initial British response to the collapse of Soviet power was 'Options For Change' published in 1990, a plan for major restructuring of all three services. In Scotland this saw the creation in 1994 of The Highlanders by amalgamation of The Queen's Own Highlanders and The Gordons. A new government then initiated the 'Strategic Defence Review' of 1998. This left the Regular

infantry intact; but the British Army retains an unusually high percentage of infantry due to the Northern Ireland commitment. Should the much-heralded 'peace process' actually evolve into a lasting cessation of violence, the Council of Scottish Colonels may face another round of painful decisions. A major factor influencing any decision on the future of Scotland's regiments will be the country's continued disproportionate contribution to the Army: 13% of Regular soldiers and 12% of Territorials, from a population that is 9% of that of the United Kingdom.

* * *

The definition of a Scottish regiment can be debatable, whether based on tradition or recruiting area. While some are self-evident, others are open to challenge. In this book we limit ourselves to The Royal Scots Dragoon Guards, The Scots Guards, and the six infantry regiments of the Scottish Division. In addition we look briefly at the Territorial Army infantry and cavalry regiments. Excluded, for example, is 1st Royal Tank Regiment, which through its recent amalgamation with 4 RTR has taken on some of that regiment's Scottish traditions including its pipe band. Equally, there is no space for the two Scottish regiments of the Royal Artillery, 19th and 40th, titled as Highland and Lowland respectively.

The abbreviations used in this text are as follows:

Regular Army

The Royal Scots Dragoon Guards	SCOTS DG
1st Bn., The Scots Guards	1 SG
The Royal Scots	1 RS
The Royal Highland Fusiliers	1 RHF
The King's Own Scottish Borderers	1 KOSB
The Black Watch	1 BW
The Argyll & Sutherland Highlanders	1 A&SH
The Highlanders	1 HLDRS

Territorial Army

Queen's Own Scottish Yeomanry	SCOTS YEO
The Lowland Volunteers	LOWLAND
3rd (Volunteer) Bn., The Royal Highland Fusiliers	3 RHF
3rd (V) Bn., The Black Watch	3 BW
3rd (V) Bn., The Highlanders	3 HLDRS
7/8th (V) Bn., The Argyll & Sutherland Highlanders	7/8 A&SH

THE ARMY IN SCOTLAND

Scotland, alongside London and the UK Support Command (Germany), is one of the three remaining districts that come under HQ UK Land Command. The District Headquarters are at Army HQ Scotland based at Craigiehall, just outside Edinburgh. Commanded by a major-general, this headquarters is responsible for the operational readiness, training and administration of all Regular, Territorial and Army Cadet Force units in Scotland. Excluded are some Army establishments including the Army Training Regiment at Glencourse. With over 1,700 Regular and 6,900 TA soldiers and 8,500 cadets, command is exercised through two brigades, each carrying the number of one of their illustrious divisional predecessors of the World Wars.

In the north is 51 Highland Brigade, based in Perth and with one Regular battalion, at Fort George, and currently three (reducing

(**Opposite**) Exhausted but jubilant Guardsmen of G Coy., 2 SG celebrate one of the fiercest actions of the Falklands War in 1982, when Scots Guards captured the heights of Mount Tumbledown from Argentinean marines - some of their best troops. Assaulting up steep slopes at night under artillery and heavy machine gun fire, 2 SG finally cleared the enemy from the hill at bayonet point. Note the piper, identified by his plain dark blue glengarry bonnet. (Soldier Magazine)

(**Above**) On 28 February 1991, under a St.Andrew's cross (saltire) pennant, the crew of a Challenger 1 Main Battle Tank from The Royal Scots Dragoon Guards rest amongst the debris of the Basra Road after a victorious four-day, 300-kilometre drive through Iraqi positions. In the process the 1st (UK) Armoured Division destroyed most of three Iraqi armoured divisions and took more than 7,000 prisoners. (US Navy)

(**Right**) Instead of the regulation Royal Tank Regiment black beret, this senior NCO from 4 RTR in the early 1990s wears the RTR badge on a glengarry, and his regiment's blue cravat. Formed by the amalgamation of 4 and 7 RTR in 1959, 4 RTR was the Scottish tank regiment; but was itself merged with 1 RTR in 1993. The new 1 RTR retains some of these links, including recruiting in Scotland and maintaining a pipe band.

to one) TA infantry battalions. In addition (prior to the current reorganization) there were three other major TA units of engineer, transport and medical troops. One responsibility is the provision of the Royal Guard for Royal visits to Balmoral each summer.

The south is covered by 52 Lowland Brigade with two Regular infantry battalions and seven major TA units including The Queen's Own Scottish Yeomanry and two infantry battalions - again, facing substantial cuts. Being based in Scotland's capital of Edinburgh, the headquarters is responsible for many ceremonial occasions including State and Royal visits

INFANTRY BATTALION - ARMOURED

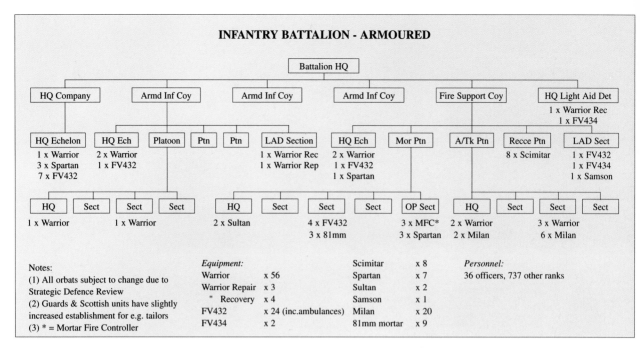

Battalion HQ

- HQ Company
- Armd Inf Coy
- Armd Inf Coy
- Armd Inf Coy
- Fire Support Coy
- HQ Light Aid Det
  - 1 x Warrior Rec
  - 1 x FV434

HQ Company:
- HQ Echelon — 1 x Warrior, 3 x Spartan, 7 x FV432
  - HQ — 1 x Warrior
  - Sect
  - Sect — 1 x Warrior
  - Sect
- HQ Ech — 2 x Warrior, 1 x FV432
- Platoon
- Ptn
- Ptn
- LAD Section — 1 x Warrior Rec, 1 x Warrior Rep

Armd Inf Coy:
- HQ Ech — 2 x Warrior, 1 x FV432, 1 x Spartan
  - HQ — 2 x Sultan
  - Sect
  - Sect
  - Sect
- Mor Ptn
  - 4 x FV432, 3 x 81mm
  - OP Sect — 3 x MFC*, 3 x Spartan

Fire Support Coy:
- A/Tk Ptn
  - HQ — 2 x Warrior, 2 x Milan
  - Sect
  - Sect — 3 x Warrior, 6 x Milan
  - Sect
- Recce Ptn — 8 x Scimitar
- LAD Sect — 1 x FV432, 1 x FV434, 1 x Samson

Notes:
(1) All orbats subject to change due to Strategic Defence Review
(2) Guards & Scottish units have slightly increased establishment for e.g. tailors
(3) * = Mortar Fire Controller

Equipment:			
Warrior	x 56	Scimitar	x 8
Warrior Repair	x 3	Spartan	x 7
" Recovery	x 4	Sultan	x 2
FV432	x 24 (inc.ambulances)	Samson	x 1
FV434	x 2	Milan	x 20
		81mm mortar	x 9

Personnel:
36 officers, 737 other ranks

INFANTRY BATTALION - MECHANIZED

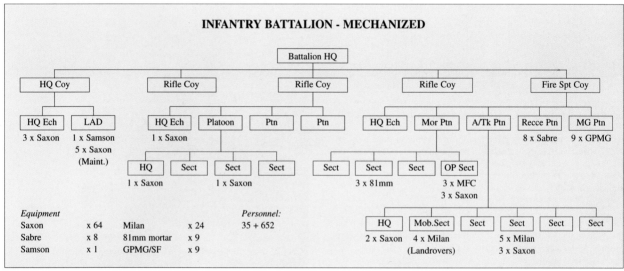

Battalion HQ

- HQ Coy
  - HQ Ech — 3 x Saxon
  - LAD — 1 x Samson, 5 x Saxon (Maint.)
- Rifle Coy
  - HQ Ech — 1 x Saxon
  - Platoon
    - HQ — 1 x Saxon
    - Sect
    - Sect — 1 x Saxon
    - Sect
  - Ptn
  - Ptn
- Rifle Coy
- Rifle Coy
  - HQ Ech
  - Mor Ptn
    - Sect
    - Sect
    - Sect — 3 x 81mm
    - OP Sect — 3 x MFC, 3 x Saxon
  - A/Tk Ptn
    - HQ — 2 x Saxon
    - Mob.Sect — 4 x Milan (Landrovers)
    - Sect
    - Sect — 5 x Milan, 3 x Saxon
    - Sect
    - Sect
  - Recce Ptn — 8 x Sabre
  - MG Ptn — 9 x GPMG
- Fire Spt Coy

Equipment				
Saxon	x 64	Milan	x 24	
Sabre	x 8	81mm mortar	x 9	
Samson	x 1	GPMG/SF	x 9	

Personnel:
35 + 652

INFANTRY BATTALION - LIGHT

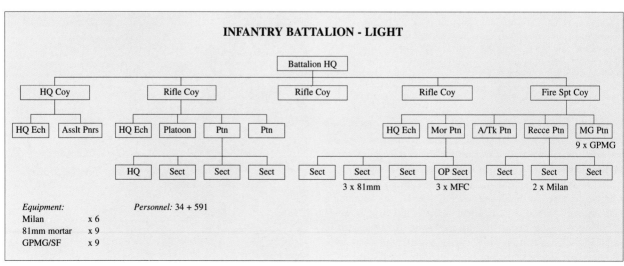

Battalion HQ

- HQ Coy
  - HQ Ech
  - Asslt Pnrs
- Rifle Coy
  - HQ Ech
  - Platoon
    - HQ
    - Sect
    - Sect
    - Sect
  - Ptn
  - Ptn
- Rifle Coy
- Rifle Coy
  - HQ Ech
  - Mor Ptn
    - Sect
    - Sect
    - Sect — 3 x 81mm
    - OP Sect — 3 x MFC
  - A/Tk Ptn
  - Recce Ptn
    - Sect
    - Sect
    - Sect — 2 x Milan
  - MG Ptn — 9 x GPMG
- Fire Spt Coy

Equipment:	
Milan	x 6
81mm mortar	x 9
GPMG/SF	x 9

Personnel: 34 + 591

(**Above**) Showing the flag means both the Scottish standard and the Union Jack for 1 RHF, serving in Bosnia as part of Operation Grapple 5 in 1995. British troops were first committed to Bosnia-Herzegovina in 1993 as part of UNPROFOR, and after the Dayton Accords of 1995 joined the NATO-led Implementation Force, I-FOR. With over 4,000 troops in theatre Britain took command of the south-west sector with headquarters at Gornji Vakuf. In contrast with the previous deployments, which had been hamstrung by a very limited UN mandate, this proved very successful. NATO agreed that a Stabilization Force, S-FOR, should succeed I-FOR when its mandate ended in December 1996. During these tours the Warrior mechanized combat vehicle - initially painted UN white but later reverting to its normal camouflage to emphasize NATO's more aggressive stance - has earned praise for its mobility and protection, not least against the ever-present threat of anti-tank mines. (1 RHF)

year later 15 Brigade, with its headquarters in York, will also transfer as its current parent - Headquarters 2 Division based at Imphal Barracks, York - closes down. On the same date, 1 April 2000, Army Headquarters Scotland will reform as Headquarters 2 (Northern) Division at its current home, Craigiehall. It is ironic that as Scotland gains greater autonomy and its own parliament, its military headquarters will assume responsibility not just for Scotland but for the north of England as well, including the two brigades and administrative control of what is now the UK's largest garrison town, Catterick.

The six Scottish infantry regiments, with their Regular and TA battalions, form an administrative grouping, the Scottish Division, which has its HQ at Edinburgh Castle.

Recruiting

Soldiers for the Scottish Division will start their careers alongside recruits for The King's Division at the Army Training Regiment, Glencourse, just south of Edinburgh. Recently introduced changes reflect the reducing levels of physical fitness of today's youth and the pressure not to waste any potential recruit. Normally, after successfully passing a 24-hour Recruit Selection Course, they have the opportunity to attend a three-week Army Foundation Course which gives them a chance to develop physical stamina and motivation while adapting to

and the guard at the Castle. An annual event now firmly established in the capital's calendar is the Edinburgh Military Tattoo, a three-week spectacle involving over 1,000 performers from around the world but centred on displays by the massed pipes and drums of the Scottish regiments.

As part of the UK Land Restructuring initiated by the Strategic Defence Review, Army Headquarters Scotland takes command of 42 Brigade, with headquarters in Preston, Lancashire, and currently part of 5 Division, in April 1999. A

(Above) The success of peace-keeping operations rests in the hands of young soldiers, junior NCOs and junior officers - whether in Bosnia or elsewhere. As part of a 'hearts and minds' campaign a corporal from The Royal Scots Dragoon Guards, with a young interpreter sporting a Worcestershire & Sherwood Foresters' sweatshirt, listens to the story of a local in the Mrkonjic Grad market - the old man had hidden with his son in caves for over four months when the town was occupied by Croats.

(Left) Two regiments of gunners show allegiance to Scotland: 19 and 40 Field Regiments Royal Artillery, the 'Highland Gunners' and 'Lowland Gunners' respectively. Here a crew from 19 Regt. prepare a 105mm Light Gun to be lifted by an RAF Chinook as they exercise alongside their fellow jocks from 1 RS in 24 Airmobile Brigade. (VS-Books/Carl Schulze)

Army life. This prepares them for the next twelve weeks, during which they complete the Common Military Syllabus (Recruits).

To attract potential recruits directly they leave school at 16 without the risk of them finding alternative careers before they are old enough to join the Army at the normal age of 16½, the Scottish Division introduced the Scottish School Leavers Scheme. This entails a 33-week course, including five weeks leave, which encompasses National Vocational Qualifications and adventure training as well as completion of the CMS(R). Currently open to those who wish to join The Scots Guards as well as the Scottish infantry regiments, this scheme has achieved such success that it has been adopted nationally, and Scotland's scheme becomes SLS (North).

While the Scottish School Leavers Scheme has been open to recruits for The Scots Guards, these would normally join others from the Guards Division at the ATR Pirbright; recruits for The Royal Scots Dragoon Guards attend the ATR Winchester, alongside others from The Royal Armoured Corps.

(**Above**) Some of the over 100 tracked vehicles that constitute a battle group. British Army Training Unit Suffield (BATUS) in Canada, with its permanent establishment of equipment ranging from Challenger 1, Warrior and artillery through to Land Rovers and trucks, hosts up to six 'Medicine Man' battle group exercises each year. For units such as 1 RHF, visiting Suffield in 1996, it is an invaluable opportunity to practice the full battalion in battle procedures over a wide area with live firing of all weapons. (1 RHF)

(**Right**) Territorial Army major from the Argylls acting as a watchkeeper during Exercise Bonny Dundee. He is a member of the District Specialist Training Team for Scotland, and wears the district patch below his regiment's distinctive flash - a strip of red and white dicing with green stripes at each end. (M.Owens/ Army HQ Scotland)

(**Left**) One strength of the British Army's regimental system which has always been particularly noted in the Scottish regiments is the strong sense of continuity across generations, with sons following fathers, brothers and uncles into the same units. This corporal from the island of Bute is the fourth generation of his family to have joined the Argylls.

The CMS(R) course covers the basic skills that all soldiers require. It starts with dress, drill, recognition of rank, and familiarity with the SA80 (L85A1) rifle before building up to fieldcraft, range work, and living in the field. Subjects like map reading, first aid and tactics are covered. Given the poor fitness levels of many of today's school leavers physical training is progressive, gradually building up strength and stamina before tackling the Basic Fitness Test or the assault course. While helicopters, wheeled or tracked vehicles may often carry today's infantry into battle, the ability to march long and hard is still vital; youths brought up wearing soft trainers and taking little exercise many face problems when they first encounter intense physical activity and Army boots. A week of adventure training helps develop the individual's confidence to face and conquer new challenges. Two important parades mark progress: the first, 'Passing Off the Square' after four weeks, allows the recruit to march about on his own and not as part of a squad. The final 'Passing Out Parade', in front of a visiting senior officer, ends the course and is held in the presence of invited family and friends - a moment of pride and satisfaction for all.

Special-to-Arm training for the infantry is carried out at the Infantry Training Centre, Catterick. Here the Combat Infantryman Course lasts another twelve weeks (except for Guardsmen, who benefit from an additional two weeks to bring them up to the high standard of drill required for public duties). For the infantryman completion of the CIC allows him to take his place confidently in a rifle section, competent in the use of the L85A1 and Light Support Weapon, in fieldcraft and tactics. Then his training really starts.

Troopers from The Royal Scots Dragoon Guards move to the Royal Armoured Corps centre at Bovington Camp in Dorset for their specialist Phase 2 training.

Light Battalions

The British Army operates a system of regular rotation through the different infantry roles; in this way an individual battalion will alternate over a number of years between the heavy armoured infantry, airmobile, and light infantry roles. Long-service soldiers thus build up an unequalled breadth of experience in military skills. The three Scottish battalions based in Scotland and the one at Catterick are currently designated as 'light infantry battalions', and are not committed to specific operational formations as are the armoured and airmobile battalions. This does not mean they suffer any less from the 'overstretch' of the Army as a whole.

They are tasked on a three-year cycle. The first is devoted to training, priority being given to training and exercises, at home and abroad, to hone individual and collective skills. This is followed by an 'operations' year, which takes priority over but does not exclude training. It is during this phase that the battalion would expect to take on the six-month role of 'Roulement Battalion' in Northern Ireland. The final year is spent on 'stand-by', on call for operations, e.g. as the Stand-by Battalion for Northern Ireland, or to support another unit in their training phase by providing enemy.

Northern Ireland

Even though the tension in Northern Ireland is perceptibly less since the major terrorist organisations declared their recent cease-fire, the British Army maintains a large, though now reducing presence there to support this peace process. The commitment is met by a mix of means. There are six resident infantry battalions posted for a two-year accompanied tour. 'Roulement battalions' (mostly of infantry, but one is usually an armoured or artillery regiment in the infantry role) rotate through on six-month unaccompanied postings. Finally, stand-by battalions are on call to be flown over as the tactical situation requires.

(**Above**) An instructor from the Royal Scots - identified by the patch of Hunting Stewart tartan worn (without a badge when in the field) on his khaki TOS - checks on the progress of two recruits as they shelter under their first *basha*, made from DPM ponchos and bungee cords. The yellow slides on their shoulder straps indicate that they are still in their first four weeks and have yet to 'Pass Off the Square'.

(**Right**) Identified by the crown and crossed flags above his chevrons of rank as an ACIO-based recruiting sergeant, this Scots Guards NCO chats to young recruits. Only 16 years old, they have been sworn in as members of the Scottish School Leavers Scheme, open to those wishing to join the Scots Guards or regiments of the Scottish Division. All regiments invest considerable effort in recruiting, supplementing the Army's centralised activities and those of local Army Career Information Offices (ACIO), as can be seen here from the additional presence of a Guardsman and piper. This scheme places another burden on often-overworked units, but the results can make the investment worth while. (M.Owens/Army HQ Scotland)

(Left) The insignia of ATR Glencourse combines those of the two administrative divisions which it serves: the Scottish (a lion rampant on the saltire), and the King's (the Tudor rose). The crossed rifles indicate the 'skill at arms' qualification. All junior NCO instructors at ATRs have passed the Section Commander's Battle Course at Infantry Training Centre (Wales), Brecon.

Civilians are sometimes puzzled by the dual meanings of the term 'division' in British Army usage. Each infantry regiment is permanently part of an administrative division - the Guards, Scottish, Queen's, King's, Prince of Wales's and Light Divisions. But these are not tactical formations which take the field together; for operational purposes units are simultaneously attached to numbered tactical brigades and divisions.

(Above) The Passing Out Parade marks successful completion of CMS(R), and the recruits' families and friends are strongly encouraged to attend. As they have yet to receive all their regiments' No.2 Dress, recruits wear a common uniform specific to ATR Glencourse: trews in regimental tartan, 'Scottish Pattern' jacket, and glengarry with their own regimental badge. This contrasts with their kilted corporal instructor from The Argyll & Sutherland Highlanders.

THE ROYAL SCOTS DRAGOON GUARDS (Carabiniers and Greys)

Currently based in Germany at Wessex Barracks, Fallingbostel, The Royal Scots Dragoon Guards are Scotland's only Regular cavalry regiment. Until recently SCOTS DG was a Type 38 armoured regiment, equipped with 38 Challenger 1 MBTs; but under recent changes it has not only received the improved Challenger 2, but also becomes a Type 58 regiment, bringing a considerable enhancement of 24 tanks. While sharing a name with its predecessor Challenger 2 is effectively a new MBT, with only 3% commonality with Challenger 1. It has much improved mobility, fire controls and reliability.

To complement this the regiment has a purpose-built training centre with state-of-the-art simulators for the instruction of loaders, gunners and commanders in the operation of equipment and software within the turret. This allows training better paced to the individual requirements of each crew member, and is available 24 hours a day, seven days a week - unlike 'real' tanks or training areas. Currently the regiment is in the process of training and working up, to become operational with Challenger 2 in 2000. As part of this process it will carry out a battle group exercise in 1999 with C Company, 2nd Bn., The Royal Regiment of Fusiliers at BATUS in Canada, the first such exercise since receipt of Challenger 2.

The regiment was created in 1971 by the amalgamation of The 3rd Carabiniers (Prince of Wales's Dragoon Guards) and The Royal Scots Greys (2nd Dragoons) - the latter being the oldest surviving Line cavalry regiment. Originally raised in 1678 as three independent troops of Scots Dragoons to suppress the Covenanters, it became the Royal Regiment of Scots Dragoons on expansion in 1681. It was shortly after this that the regiment began to be mounted on the grey horses which would bring them their traditional title, and which would make such an impression on Napoleon himself during their famous charge at Waterloo on 18 June 1815. While the Carabiniers were firmly based south of the border at Chester, the new amalgamated regiment yielded none of its Scottish character while adopting some of the English customs. With its Home Headquarters at Edinburgh Castle, the SCOTS DG recruits from across Scotland.

Recent service

In 1961 the Carabiniers had a taste of things to come when they were rushed to Kuwait to deter a threatened Iraqi invasion. Thirty years later, in Operation Granby, their successors deployed to Saudi Arabia as part of 7 Armoured Brigade in response to an actual invasion. Extensive desert training followed; at that time the Challenger 1 MBT had a worrying reputation for unreliability. However, when the ultimate test of battle came the tank passed triumphantly. Under intensive use in the harshest terrain and climate, good maintenance by its crews and attached REME personnel - and logistical support on a war footing, without peacetime constraints - allowed Challenger to prove itself well up to the job.

By the time Desert Shield (as the Americans called the operation) switched to the offensive and Desert Storm, the initial

(Above) In Bosnia the Challenger 1, battle-proven as the SCOTS DGs' mount in the Gulf War, provided the 'big stick' to keep the warring factions apart. The TOGS housing (Thermal Observation & Gunnery System) bears the St.Andrew's Cross (saltire) and the insignia of 7 Armoured Brigade - the red jerboa 'desert rat' made famous by 7th Armoured Division in the Second World War. The troopers' grey berets recall the Scots Greys, and bear on a black backing the badge of a French Imperial eagle (commemorating that captured by Sgt.Ewart of the Scots Greys from the French 45th Infantry Regiment at Waterloo) over crossed carbines from the badge of the former 3rd Carabiniers.

British brigade had grown to 1st (UK) Armoured Division. Attacking as part of US XVIII Corps, the UK division exploited initial breaches in Iraqi defences with 7 Armoured Brigade in the van. The British armour wheeled to attack the Iraqi 12th Tank Division, and initial weak resistance soon stiffened as the SCOTS DG Battle Group advanced on a large enemy communications complex. Helped by their attached Warrior-borne infantry company from 1st Bn., The Staffordshire Regiment, the SCOTS DG cleared this objective in appalling conditions of rain and darkness. Thus the first day, Sunday 24 February 1991, drew to a close. By the Wednesday it was all over: the Iraqis had been routed. In less than four days 1st (UK) Armoured Division had advanced nearly 150 miles, fighting most of the way.

(Above) A mounted escort from SCOTS DG was part of the procession which on St.Andrew's Day, 30 November 1997, carried the Stone of Destiny home to Edinburgh Castle. Riding greys, the officer and troopers wear the scarlet of British heavy cavalry with yellow facings inherited from the 3rd Dragoon Guards; the double stripe on the blue overalls recalls the Carabiniers. From the Greys comes the bearskin, unique amongst British cavalry, marking the defeat of the French *Régiment de Roi* at Ramillies in 1706.

(Left) HM The Queen, Colonel-in-Chief of the regiment, presents a new standard. Note the badge of the Prince of Wales's plumes on the bearer's left sleeve; this comes from the old 3rd Dragoon Guards, honoured with the title Prince of Wales's since 1765. The officer's No.1 Dress cap, left, bears the Scots Greys' traditional yellow 'vandyked' band. (Capt.R.Clayton/ SCOTS DG)

Regimental lineage

The Royal Scots Greys (2nd Dragoons) Raised 1678; 1681, Royal Regiment of Scots Dragoons; 1751, 2nd Royal North British Dragoons.

The 3rd Carabiniers (Prince of Wales's Dragoon Guards) Formed 1922 as 3rd/6th Dragoon Guards - taking the above title in 1928 - by amalgamation of *3rd Dragoon Guards (Prince of Wales's),* raised 1685 as the Earl of Plymouth's Regiment of Horse; and the *Carabiniers (6th Dragoon Guards),* raised in the same year, as the Queen Dowager's Horse.

   The amalgamated regiment of 1971 is the heir to some 90 battle honours since 1701, including Blenheim, Dettingen, Warburg, Albuhera, Vittoria, Waterloo; Balaklava, Abyssinia; Retreat from Mons, Ypres, Cambrai, Hindenburg Line; El Alamein, Salerno, Falaise, Imphal, Nunshigum and Mandalay.

(Top & above) A mounted detachment in full dress uniform is provided for ceremonial occasions when practical. The mounts are all greys except for the drum horse, 'Ramillies' - presented by HM The Queen, this is the biggest horse in the British Army (and his drummer wears the Army's only white bearskin). (Capt.R.Clayton/ SCOTS DG)

(Right) Waiting to perform at the Edinburgh Tattoo, a SCOTS DG piper rehearses in the Castle, their Home Headquarters. The kilt, plaid (held by a silver brooch of the White Horse of Hanover) and pipes are in the Royal Stewart tartan, a privilege granted by King George VI. The doublet is dark blue; the sporran is of grey horsehair with black and red tassels - the plume colours of the old 3rd Dragoon Guards. Just visible hanging at his hip is the feather-mounted bonnet with a band of yellow vandyking. The pipers serve as tank crews like their comrades, spread between the squadrons, although as musicians they work together.

(**Above & opposite**) Challenger 2 at last gives the Royal Armoured Corps a tank fully worthy of its crews, with far better fire control and mobility. Although disguised by the rather bland outline imposed on several modern MBTs by their shroud of Chobham composite armour, Challenger 2 in fact differs in most respects from its predecessor. Pennants on the radio antennae identify SCOTS DG: one, obscured here, is in the regimental colours - narrow grey, yellow and red stripes on a dark blue ground; the other - the red lion rampant on yellow of Scotland's standard - identifies the regimental commanding officer's tank. (**Inset**) Another mark of the CO's tank is the matt green lion rampant stencilled on the turret of his Challenger 2.

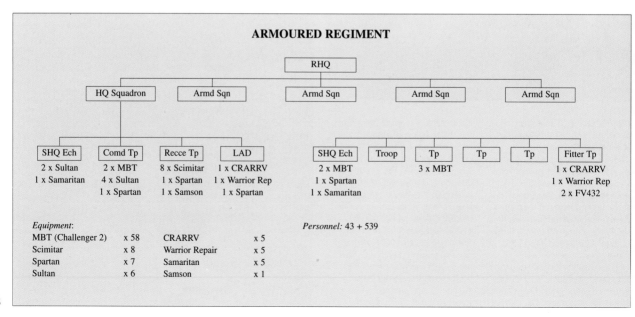

ARMOURED REGIMENT

		RHQ		
HQ Squadron	Armd Sqn	Armd Sqn	Armd Sqn	Armd Sqn

SHQ Ech	Comd Tp	Recce Tp	LAD		SHQ Ech	Troop	Tp	Tp	Tp	Fitter Tp
2 x Sultan	2 x MBT	8 x Scimitar	1 x CRARRV		2 x MBT		3 x MBT			1 x CRARRV
1 x Samaritan	4 x Sultan	1 x Spartan	1 x Warrior Rep		1 x Spartan					1 x Warrior Rep
	1 x Spartan	1 x Samson	1 x Spartan		1 x Samaritan					2 x FV432

Equipment:

MBT (Challenger 2)	x 58		CRARRV	x 5
Scimitar	x 8		Warrior Repair	x 5
Spartan	x 7		Samaritan	x 5
Sultan	x 6		Samson	x 1

Personnel: 43 + 539

(Above) On the final range before the return of the regiment's Challenger 1s, troopers of SCOTS DG prepare the charges and practice HESH rounds for the 120mm main armament. Known as 'shush-p' from its official name of 'SH/Prac', and coloured blue like all practice rounds, it is an inert solid shot with tracer to track its flight.

(Left) One of the promises of Challenger 2 is greater reliability and maintainability, although it is doubtful whether the workload for the REME craftsmen of the SCOTS DG Light Aid Detachment will be much reduced. While retaining their own corps cap badge these attached personnel show allegiance to the regiment by wearing it on the grey beret.

(**Above & right**) While Challenger 1 is being replaced by Challenger 2 the rest of the regiment's armoured vehicles remain from earlier generations. Here signallers monitor the net in one of the regimental command element's Sultan armoured command vehicles, a variant of the CVR(T) series. Note the 7 Armoured Brigade 'desert rat' sleeve patch.

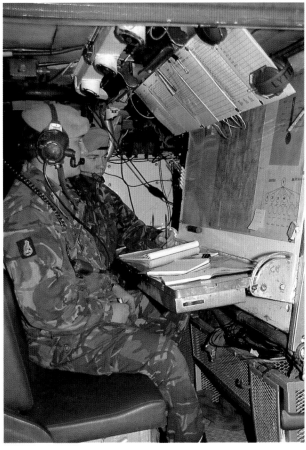

(**Above**) Despite its age the Scimitar CVR(T) remains an effective reconnaissance vehicle, reasonably well protected and well armed with its 30mm Rarden cannon. It is very fast, and highly mobile due to its excellent flotation (low weight spread over wide track contact area). This mobility was to prove useful when SCOTS DG deployed to Bosnia as part of S-FOR, becoming responsible for an area 135km from north to south and up to 80km wide, in terrain up to 6,000ft high, with many very marginal roads and weak bridges.

(**Left**) Security at the SCOTS DG regimental base at the Mrkonjic Grad bus depot in Bosnia was a continual problem; the threat was not so much from enemy fire as from perpetual attempts at theft. Guard dogs, mainly German Shepherds, proved a valuable deterrent, with the handlers volunteering for duty and passing a course run by the Royal Army Veterinary Corps at Split. As units returned to Germany the dogs would be handed on to their replacements.

(**Opposite top**) Sharing many of the automotive advances of the Challenger 2, the Challenger Armoured Repair & Recovery Vehicle (CRARRV) provides the muscle, lifting capability and mobility to the Forward Repair Teams with each squadron. It will not only extract a broken-down tank from trouble, but can carry out a complete power pack change in the field.

(**Opposite**) Modern weapons are increasingly complex systems requiring skilled and highly trained operators; and the rounds they fire are very expensive. Alongside the introduction of Challenger 2, a new dedicated training complex with simulators for loaders, gunners and commanders represents a considerable leap forward over previous training regimes. Even before they take Challenger 2 on to a training area or gunnery range the crew, such as this gunner on the Part Task Trainer, are familiar with the controls and drills.

THE SCOTS GUARDS

In 1982 the final action of the campaign to liberate the Falkland Islands from the forces of the Argentine military junta was the capture of hills protecting the approaches to Port Stanley. In a night attack on 13/14 June the 2nd Bn., Scots Guards took on one of the crack Argentine units, the 5th Marine Infantry Battalion, who were dug in among the rocks of Mount Tumbledown and nearby features in strong mutually-supporting positions. At 0030hrs an initial diversionary attack by elements of the battalion's Fire Support Company, supported by Scorpions of the Blues & Royals, occupied the Argentineans' attention; and G Coy. took their objective on the western edge of the mountain. They could then support Left Flank Coy. as they fought their way towards the summit.

Under fire from mortars, artillery, and 0.5in Browning heavy machine guns in a system of interlocking sangars, the Guardsmen faced a slow, bitter fight in the freezing darkness. Everything was thrown at the enemy; 2 SG blasted them with rounds from the 66mm LAW, 84mm Carl Gustav and M79 grenade launcher, then closed in with the hand grenade, the rifle, and finally the bayonet. They were pinned down for some time at a point where high rocks chanelled the attack into a 50-yard wide valley. Artillery support on targets only 100 yards away was skilfully controlled by the attached RA Foward Observation Officer, and another platoon attack regained the initiative. Suddenly the summit was reached, and Right Flank Coy. could take on the final phase - again, in remorseless combat which came to hand-to-hand. After repelling two counter-attacks - one by the 5th Marines and one by B Coy./6th Infantry Regiment - the battalion were finally secure on Tumbledown by 0820hrs, and their opponents could be seen streaming back to Port Stanley. Scots Guards casualties were nine dead and 41 wounded. This hard-fought battle was won by the courage and initiative of the junior ranks, pressing forward in small groups, even alone, to take the fight to the enemy. It was recognized by the award of the battle honour Tumbledown Mountain.

Unfortunately this was not enough to save the 2nd Battalion from Army reductions; in 1993 it was placed in 'suspended animation', and is now represented by F Coy., Scots Guards, who carry the colours. Based at Wellington Barracks, London, and administered by 1st Bn., Welsh Guards, they have an establishment of five officers and 100 other ranks, carrying out public duties as required by HQ London District.

Meanwhile, in a typically radical change from their last tour - public duties at Victoria Barracks, Windsor - the 1st Battalion are half way through a two-year tour in Northern Ireland. Based at Ballykinler, they work in four company groupings: one in South Armagh, one as Province reserve, one on barrack duties and leave, and the last training, on stand-by, and recruiting back in Scotland.

Part of The Household Division, The Scots Guards have their Regimental Headquarters in London and a Home Headquarters at Edinburgh Castle, recruiting from Scotland and the north of England.

Regimental lineage

The history of the regiment spans over 350 years' proud service to the Crown. Raised in 1642 as a Royal Guard for Charles I, they fought Irish rebels for seven years while the English Civil War raged at home. Back in Scotland they transferred their allegiance to the fugitive Charles II on the execution of Charles I in 1649. After the Royalist army's final defeat by Cromwell at Worcester in 1651 they disbanded. With Charles II's restoration a company of guards was raised in Edinburgh in October 1660, and another shortly afterwards at Dumbarton. A Royal Warrent of 1662 directed the raising of additional companies, to be entitled the Scots Regiment of Guards. They moved from the Scottish to the English establishment in 1686. Various changes of title followed, including for many years 3rd Foot Guards; and it was not until 1877 that they became simply The Scots Guards.

The regiment has earned over 90 battle honours since Namur 1695, including Dettingen, Talavera, Fuentes d'Onor, Salamanca, Waterloo; Inkerman, Egypt 1882, Modder River; Marne 1914, Ypres, Festubert, Loos, Somme; Norway 1940, Tobruk 1941, Gazala, Salerno, Anzio, Venlo Pocket and Reichswald.

(Opposite) A Company Sergeant Major lays a wreath at The Scots Guards Memorial in Edinburgh Castle on ANZAC Day. His three medals tell part of his story: from left to right, at least one tour in Northern Ireland, earning the General Service Medal; the Gulf War; and the Long Service & Good Conduct Medal, for over 15 years' service with the colours. The peak of his forage cap is 'slashed' in The Scots Guards' customary manner so that it rests just above the bridge of the nose. (M.Owens/Army HQ Scotland)

(Above & right) Ceremonial occasions such as the annual Trooping of the Colour - the Queen's Birthday Parade - on Horseguards Parade in London each June require considerable rehearsal. For this supreme moment of British military pageantry the highest standards of precision and turn-out are expected (not least by that most knowledgeable of judges, Her Majesty The Queen). Here Scots Guards practice at Pirbright in Barrack Dress Drill Order, with officers and Guardsmen in their bearskins and senior NCOs, as a privilege, in the regiment's distinctive forage cap. The bearskins have to be worn for rehearsals to ensure proper sizing of the Guardsmen in their ranks.

(Above) The old Guard stand at ease in front of the Guard Room at Windsor Castle waiting for the sentries to be changed as part of the Guard Mount; the two waiting Captains of the Guard 'pace the minutes', marching back and forth. The bugler's and drummer's tunics are trimmed with distinctive 'drummer's lace', a pattern of blue *fleurs de lis* on white.

(Left) The public's usual view of members of the Foot Guards regiments – which can be deceptive, unless one notices the active service medals worn by many. This sentry stands at ease outside his box at Windsor. The bearskin was adopted in 1831; while the Grenadiers and Coldstream wore respectively red and white plumes on the bearskin the 3rd Guards, as the most junior and 'centre of the line', chose not to. Their place in the precedence of the Foot Guards is reflected in the grouping of tunic buttons in threes. The sentry will be on duty for two hours followed by a minimum break of four hours. As often as he feels the need he may 'patrol', marching a set number of paces to left or right.

(Opposite top) Scots Guardsmen take each other at mutual drill in order to develop their word of command. Part of the battalion's junior NCO cadre, they wear Barrack Dress Drill Order as they work under the critical eye of their sergeant Drill Instructor. By the end of the course their uniform will, if necessary, be exchanged or altered to meet the high standard expected of a junior NCO in the Guards - a possible explanation for the missing forage cap of the Guardsman in the beret.

(Right & far right) Detail differences between the mess kits of officers (left) and senior NCOs include the collar badges - the Star of the Order of the Thistle for the officer and a thistle for the colour-sergeant. Worn on the right sleeve only, the rank badge from the mess kit of a Scots Guards colour-sergeant is smaller than that worn on Full Dess; the chevrons are overlaid with a representation of the original 'colour badge' of 1813 - a crown over a single colour, here showing the Order of the Thistle, with crossed swords.

(Above) Pipers from the Pipes and Drums of the SG in their Full Dress uniforms wear a kilt and plaid in Royal Stewart tartan with hose of red and green marl. Their black feather bonnet carries a hackle of blue over red.

(Above right) An off-duty piper carries kilt and doublet while wearing trews in Royal Stewart tartan; his glengarry - for all Scottish pipers, plain dark blue without dicing - bears an enlarged version of the badge: the Star of the Order of the Thistle, surrounded by the regimental title.

(Right) At the entrance to Victoria Barracks, Windsor, a Guardsman and an attached lance-corporal from the Royal Army Medical Corps provide security. They wear Patrol Order with the Combat 95 Body Armour for protection, and the khaki beret of the Guards. Cap badges are mounted on the blue and red striped flash of the Household Division, while that of the RAMC is backed by an additional dull cherry flash. Officers in The Scots Guards wear instead a Royal Stewart tartan flash behind their badge.

(See also Europa-Militaria No.20: *The Guards - Britain's Household Division*)

THE ROYAL SCOTS (The Royal Regiment)

The Royal Scots, based at Hyderabad Barracks in Colchester, are currently one of 24 Airmobile Brigade's two infantry battalions. The brigade is designated to the Multi-National Division (Central) – M.N.D.(C) – the airmobile division of NATO's Allied Rapid Reaction Corps. Part of the role of the brigade is to act as a flexible, mobile counter-penetration force able to deploy anywhere within the NATO area. In the purely British context it would form a valuable asset for the Joint Rapid Deployment Force.

What distinguishes the airmobile battalion is its ability to deploy, sustain operations for up to 48 hours, and then be resupplied by air. While the method of deployment may be different the concept of operations is similar to that of 5 Airborne Brigade (and both have a very high scale of Milan anti-tank guided weapons). It is therefore unsurprising that under the Strategic Defence Review these two formations are to merge to form 16 Air Assault Brigade (the final title has yet to be announced, but it may be called after the famous 16 Parachute Brigade disbanded in 1976). The new formation is planned to operate with a strong Army Air Corps force of Apache Longbow attack helicopters.

This role is in stark contrast to 1991 when the battalion, then serving as armoured infantry, deployed to the Gulf from Germany with 45 Warrior mechanized combat vehicles as part of 4 Armoured Brigade. When the ground offensive to liberate Kuwait opened at 2a.m. on 24 February 1991, 1 RS began a hectic 96 hours as 1st (UK) Armoured Division cut a swathe through successive Iraqi brigade positions codenamed 'Bronze', 'Brass' and 'Tungsten'. Within the first day the Royal Scots destroyed an artillery battery, and the following day overran more gun positions at Wadi al Batin, capturing many prisoners. Assaults were mounted both aboard their Warriors, using the 30mm Rarden cannon and 7.62mm chain gun; and dismounted, using Milan as a very effective 'bunker buster', followed up with rifle and grenade.

Edinburgh Castle houses the Regimental Headquarters, with recruits being sought from the capital and the neighbouring areas of Lothian and Tweedale.

(**Top right**) In a flurry of snow a piper plays. The tartan is Royal Stewart, first permitted in 1933 on the occasion of the Royal Scots' tercentenary. Behind the badge - the Star of the Order of the Thistle with St.Andrew and Cross - he wears blackcock feathers.

(**Centre right**) A patch of Hunting Stewart tartan is worn by 1 RS behind the cap badge on the tam-o'-shanter.

(**Right**) Gurkha soldier of B Coy., 1 RS; he retains the cap badge of The Royal Gurkha Rifles on a patch of the Royal Scots' Hunting Stewart tartan.

Regimental lineage

The regiment was raised by Sir John Hepburn in 1633 by Royal Warrant from Charles I of England and Scotland for service with the French Crown, and so can claim the honour of being Britain's oldest surviving regiment and senior regiment of infantry. They became Douglas's Regiment in 1637, the Scotch Regiment of Foot in 1666, and the Earl of Dumbarton's Regiment in 1678. (Legend has it that the nickname 'Pontius Pilate's Bodyguard' arose from a dispute over precedence with the French *Régiment de Picardie* as early as 1643.)

Although officially brought into the British establishment in 1661 the unit did not return until 1678. In 1684 they became the Royal Regiment of Foot, and claimed the place of honour at the right of the line of the Royal army of James II when it defeated the rebel Duke of Monmouth at the battle of Sedgemoor in 1685. With the Glorious Revolution of 1688 they remained loyal to their king until the departure of James II and his fellow Roman Catholic the Earl of Dumbarton. Required by the new Dutch monarch William III for service in Holland, they headed instead for Scotland, where the new king had yet to be accepted; overtaken by loyal troops, they were leniently treated. The regiment agreed to serve the new monarchy, and moved to Holland, not returning until 1697.

Subsequent service has taken the regiment - officially numbered the 1st or Royal Regiment of Foot since 1751 - and its battalions all over the world in all the major campaigns of the British Army. It was not until 1812 that the title 'Royal Scots' was conferred; after a brief period as The Lothian Regiment (Royal Scots) in 1881, and some forty years as The Royal Scots (Lothian Regiment), the current form was adopted in 1920. A plan to merge the regiment with The King's Own Scottish Borderers was mooted in 1991, but was abandoned in 1993. The Royal Scots have earned about 160 battle honours since Tangier 1680, including Blenheim, Havannah, Egypt, Corunna, Busaco, Niagara, Waterloo; Alma, Inkerman, Sevastopol, Pekin 1860, South Africa 1899-1902; Le Cateau, Loos, Gallipoli 1915-16, Somme 1916, Palestine 1917-18, Archangel 1918-19; Dyle, St.Omer-La Bassée, South-East Asia 1941, Odon, Caen, Nederrijn, Gothic Line, Italy 1944-45, Reichswald, and Relief of Kohima.

(**Above**) The Queen's and Regimental Colours of the 2nd Bn., Royal Scots are displayed in the Officers' Mess; as this unit amalgamated with the 1st Bn. in 1949, rather than being disbanded, the Colours were not laid up in a cathedral. Generally Queen's Colours, based on the Union Flag, bear ten representative battle honours from the First World War, ten from the Second, and selected subsequent actions. The Regimental Colours show all the battle honours awarded before the Great War.

(**Opposite top**) When the Gurkha regiments amalgamated to form The Royal Gurkha Rifles in 1994 they were cut from four to two battalions. With the surplus manpower three Gurkha Reinforcement Companies were created to supplement other regiments; 1 RS were one of the units which benefited, their Gurkhas forming B Company - a celebration of the traditionally close friendship between Scots and Gurkhas since Victorian battles in India. The Hunting Stewart flash was added to the RGR rifle-green beret and badge.

(Below) A Gurkha with the 5.56mm Light Support Weapon leads his section; each British infantry section has two LSWs, and operates as two four-man fire teams. The LSW has most components in common with the L85A1 rifle, including the 30-round magazine, but a longer, heavier barrel and a bipod. It is impressively accurate, to longer ranges than the rifle; but arguably it lacks the weight of fire needed for a section machine gun. (VS-Books/Carl Schulze)

(Below right) As part of 24th Airmobile Bde., 1 RS train with RAF Puma and Chinook helicopters and also, as here, with Lynx Mk.9s from the brigade's 3 Regiment, Army Air Corps. The Lynx provides tactical mobility, over ranges up to 120km, for up to six 'pax' - airmobile jargon for a soldier and his equipment for 48 hours' unsupported operations; this photo shows half of a six-man 'chalk' awaiting extraction. (VS-Books/Carl Schulze)

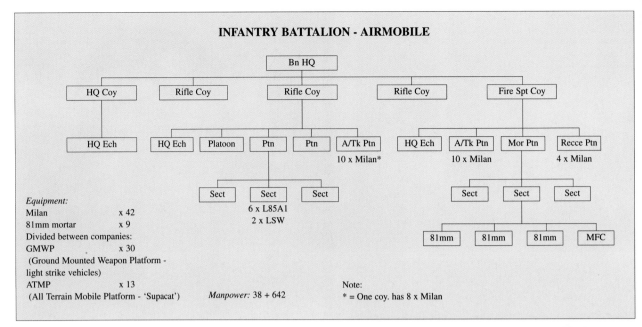

INFANTRY BATTALION - AIRMOBILE

```
                              Bn HQ
        ┌──────────┬──────────┼──────────┬──────────────┐
     HQ Coy     Rifle Coy   Rifle Coy   Rifle Coy    Fire Spt Coy
        │                       │                         │
     HQ Ech    ┌────┬──────┬────┴──┬────────┐    ┌──────┬──────┬──────┐
            HQ Ech Platoon Ptn    Ptn    A/Tk Ptn HQ Ech A/Tk Ptn Mor Ptn Recce Ptn
                                          10 x Milan*      10 x Milan  4 x Milan
                        ┌──────┼──────┐              ┌──────┼──────┐
                      Sect   Sect   Sect           Sect   Sect   Sect
                           6 x L85A1                        │
                           2 x LSW            ┌──────┬──────┼──────┐
                                            81mm   81mm   81mm   MFC
```

Equipment:
Milan   x 42
81mm mortar   x 9
Divided between companies:
GMWP   x 30
(Ground Mounted Weapon Platform -
light strike vehicles)
ATMP   x 13
(All Terrain Mobile Platform - 'Supacat')   *Manpower:* 38 + 642

Note:
* = One coy. has 8 x Milan

(Right) On the right shoulder of combat clothing 1 RS wear this patch of Hunting Stewart tartan - note that it is reversed from that worn on the headgear, with the yellow overstripe from top left to bottom right.

(Right) On the left shoulder of 'combats' all 24 Airmobile Brigade units wear the brigade insignia - red griffon's wings on dark blue, from the family crest of the Second World War Airborne Forces commander, General 'Boy' Browning.

(See also Europa-Militaria No.23:
British 24th Airmobile Brigade)

Even with a 'peace process' in progress Northern Ireland remains a major commitment for the Army, and places like Drumcree continue to be points of tension between two communities capable of exploding into violence at any moment - all too often held apart only by the security forces.

(Above) A soldier from 1 RS deploys from a Saxon patrol vehicle, specially adapted for internal security duties in the Province. (1 RS)

(Right) A jock wearing the Internal Security helmet during training in a FIBUA ('fighting in built-up areas') facility for duty in Northern Ireland.

(Above) A patrol commander briefs his men while acting as enemy on a brigade exercise - hence the badged TOSs instead of helmets. They wear the familiar temperate climate DPM combats - No.8 Dress - and the now-standard Pattern 90 Personal Load Carrying Equipment. The centre soldiers wears the latest Combat 95 ripstop combat jacket.

(Right) Two soldiers from 1 RS take a short breather while on exercise in Kenya - a welcome change from the more familiar British and European training areas. They wear the desert pattern combats, No.9 Dress, as introduced for the Gulf War, with the now-standard body armour; note smoke grenades on their webbing. While the fixed bayonet on the L85A1 may seem incongruous in the age of precision guided munitions, recent conflicts from the Falklands to the Gulf have shown its continuing value in the hands of Scottish soldiers. (1 RS)

THE ROYAL HIGHLAND FUSILIERS (Princess Margaret's Own Glasgow and Ayrshire Regiment)

On a passing-out parade at Glencourse a sergeant of the Royal Highland Fusiliers, in No.2 Dress, carries a pace stick. As well as serving in the Gulf War and Northern Ireland he has served one tour with UNPROFOR in Bosnia; the oakleaf on the medal ribbon indicates that he was awarded a Mention in Dispatches. As a corporal, he and a section of six had been occupying a position when it came under attack from a machine gun. Removing the pintle-mounted GPMG from their FV432 carrier, he and his men charged; the enemy ran ....

The second oldest of the Scottish Regiments, The Royal Highland Fusiliers was born of the amalgamation in 1959 of The Royal Scots Fusiliers, raised in 1678 as the Earl of Mar's Regiment of Foot, and The Highland Light Infantry, raised in 1777 and - despite its title - recruited from Glasgow. As with all regiments, its enormously varied historic and recent history echoes that of the British Army as a whole.

In 1946 the 1st Battalion, HLI handed over the Citadel in Cairo to the Egyptian Army, hauling down a flag that had been raised by their 2nd Battalion after the battle of Tel-el-Kebir in 1882.

When on 21 December 1988 Pan-Am Flight 103 was brought down at Lockerbie by a terrorist bomb with tragic loss of life, 1 RHF were among those called upon to help the emergency services in the task of recovering human remains. Interestingly, while some members of the emergency services required sick leave, suffered from 'post traumatic stress disorder', and sought financial compensation, the jocks quietly got on with their lives. Their contribution to this gruesome task was recognized by the award of the Wilkinson Sword of Peace.

Now an armoured infantry battalion based in Germany at St.Barbara's Barracks, Fallingbostel, 1 RHF is part of 7 Armoured Brigade, in turn part of 1 (UK) Armoured Division, Britain's principle contribution to the Allied Rapid Reaction Corps. In operations 1 RHF would fight as a battle group with at least one of its Warrior armoured infantry companies detached and replaced by an armoured squadron with tanks, giving a balanced force to suit the tactical situation.

In April 1999 they return to Bosnia as part of S-FOR's Multi-National Division (South-West) for a six-month tour, shipping their own Warriors and other vehicles. The regiment can boast of having the longest title in the British Army; and as it suggests, they recruit from Glasgow - where their RHQ is located - and Ayrshire.

(See also Europa-Militaria No.25: *Warrior Company*)

Regimental lineage

The Royal Scots Fusiliers Raised 1678 by Charles Erskine, Earl of Mar, and known as the Scots Fusiliers by 1685. The regiment fought at Walcourt and Steenkirk in the Netherlands in 1689 and 1692; and earned the nickname 'Marlborough's Own' at Blenheim, Oudenarde, Ramillies and Malplaquet in the first decade of the 18th century. Political sensitivity over Jacobite unrest led to renaming as Royal North British Fusiliers in 1713; veterans of Fontenoy (1745), the regiment became the 21st of Foot by 1751, and The Royal Scots Fusiliers in 1881.

The Highland Light Infantry Raised 1777 as the 73rd of Foot, Lord MacLeod's Highlanders; renumbered as 71st in 1786. By 1809 the regiment was retitled 71st (Glasgow) Highland Light Infantry, shortly afterwards losing the city name - but never the association, becoming The Highland Light Infantry (City of Glasgow Regiment) in 1881.

The amalgamated regiment is the heir to more than 200 battle honours (the highest number in the British Army), including Blenheim, Dettingen, Gibraltar 1780-83, Martinique, Seringapatam, Assaye, Cape of Good Hope, Rolica, Ciudad Rodrigo, Badajos, Pyrenees, Bladensburg, Waterloo; Alma, Central India, Tel-el-Kebir, Burma 1885-87, Tirah, Relief of Ladysmith; Mons, Ypres 1915, Somme 1916, Gallipoli 1915-16, Mesopotamia 1916-18, Vimy 1917, Passchendaele, St.Quentin Canal; Somme 1940, Abyssinia 1941, Gazala, Sicily 1943, Anzio, Garigliano Crossing, Falaise, Venlo Pocket, Roer, Rhineland, Greece 1944-45 and Burma 1944-45.

(Left) An RHF platoon sergeant checks his planned route on the ranges at Fallingbostel. The commercial hand-held GPS receivers bought by 7 Armoured Brigade continually prove their usefulness as an aid to navigation, whether on the featureless plains of Suffield, Canada, or when disorientated amongst the trees and sometimes blinding sand on the training areas in Germany.

(Below) One of 56 held in the battalion, the Combat Vehicle Personnel Tracked - the Warrior - is the principal vehicle of armoured infantry such as 1 RHF. They offer mobility comparable to that of the Challenger tanks they fight alongside, and adequate protection (though less than that enjoyed by an MBT). Warrior carries a total of ten men - commander, gunner, driver, and seven other soldiers. The commander dismounts with his section to work as two fire teams, leaving the driver and the gunner - the latter as vehicle commander - with the 'wagon'; they provide fire support as necessary.

The white and red lollipop-shaped Weapons State Indicators - which can be switched while closed down - indicate 'guns clear' or 'guns loaded' when field firing on ranges.

(Opposite) Clips of three blue practice rounds for the 30mm Rarden are loaded into an FV510 Warrior section vehicle by fusiliers from 1 RHF. The green flag on the turret indicates 'gun clear' and would be changed to red when loaded. The cannon and a co-axial 7.62 chain gun provide ample firepower, whether on the move or supporting dismounted infantry.

(Above) An FV432 ambulance is refuelled from a Bedford TM 8-tonne UBRE (Unit Bulk Refuelling Equiment) bowser. The venerable FV432 has been in service since the early 1960s; since being replaced as the infantry carrier by Warrior it remains valuable in many second-line roles, with little sign of early replacement. The 432 now runs on diesel, the dominant military fuel for reasons of safety and economy - few vehicles still use CIVGAS, petrol.

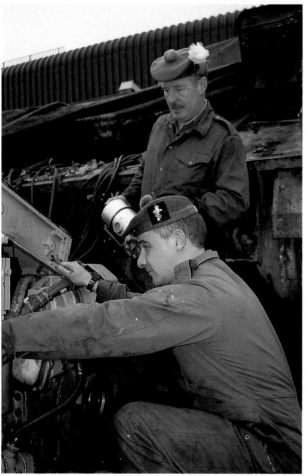

(Left) Working on a Warrior power pack, a REME craftsman of 1 RHF Light Aid Detachment (foreground) wears a TOS with tartan patch and his corps' cap badge. An LAD section of nine craftsmen with two specialist Warrior variants - one FV513 MCRV for recovery and one FV512 MRV(R) for repair - supports each of the armoured infantry companies.

(Above) A lance-corporal of 1 RHF on foot patrol in West Belfast, protecting the Royal Ulster Constabulary. As a confidence-building measure with the civil population since the ostensible cease-fire by the PIRA terrorist movement, troops patrol in regimental headgear rather than helmets - here, the khaki TOS with the white RHF hackle and a flash of Mackenzie tartan. This soldier wears chest webbing and a radio, and carries a Maglite as well as his L85A1 rifle. Note the very subdued rank insignia below his 7 Armoured Brigade patch. (1 RHF)

(Right) A fusilier wearing 'blues' - No.1 Dress - shows off the RHF's blue glengarry with diced band and grenade-shaped badge (from the old Royal Scots Fusiliers), with the monogram 'HLI' surmounted by the crown (from the old Highland Light Infantry). Grenade badges and white tufts echo the very distant days when fusiliers served as artillery guards under the Board of Ordnance .

(**Above**) Pipers practice on their chanters, the part of the pipes on which the melody is played - a simpler and quieter process than using the full set! The strip of cloth on the table is of the Dress Erskine tartan, the same as their kilts.

(**Right**) Fusiliers illustrate a selection of dress: No.2, No.1, and combats. The trews are of Mackenzie tartan, a Government or Black Watch sett with overstripes of white and red, which dates back to the 71st Highland Light Infantry and was named after their colonel when adopted. At the time of amalgamation the HLI wore the kilt in Mackenzie and the RSF were in trews of Hunting Erskine. The current dress is a careful compromise, with the pipers in archer-green doublets and kilts of Dress Erskine.

THE KING'S OWN SCOTTISH BORDERERS

The King's Own Scottish Borderers are one of only two Scottish regiments never to have been amalgamated (the other being The Black Watch). Raised in 1689 to protect Edinburgh against the Jacobites, it marched north to defeat at Killiecrankie - though it was one of only two regiments not broken by the Highlanders, and withdrew in good order. It was only renamed as The King's Own Scottish Borderers in 1887, having resisted an arbitrary attempt during the great reorganizations of 1881 to move the regimental depot to York and call it the York Regiment, King's Own Borderers. As a compromise the depot moved to Berwick-on-Tweed, which remains the Regimental Headquarters; and it is from the Borders, Dumfries and Galloway areas and parts of Lanarkshire that the regiment recruits.

After the Second World War the 2nd Battalion was disbanded in 1947, leaving the 1st Battalion to carry out the usual round of operational tours in Palestine, Singapore and Malaya, Aden and the Radfan, Sarawak, Northern Ireland (the first in 1970), and the Gulf War as the prisoner-of-war guard force. In addition they served with particular distinction in Korea.

The 1st Bn., KOSB arrived in that country in April 1951, in time for a major Communist offensive and a retreat by the United Nations forces. By late September the Commonwealth Division had once more advanced; and on 3 October the 1 KOSB captured Hill 355. This new defensive line came under sustained attack, and on the evening of Sunday 4 November a Chinese division of 6,000 men was launched against the battalion's position. After three hours of intense bombardment enemy infantry stormed the wire and trenches; some positions were overrun, and the survivors pulled back. Private William Speakman, a Cheshire man attached from The Black Watch, left his company headquarters with pockets full of grenades, "Going to shift some of those bloody chinks"; at first he was alone, but later others followed him. After repeated counter-attacks and bitter hand-to-hand fighting, by dawn the hill was back in the possession of 1 KOSB. The enemy left some 1,000 dead, for the loss to the Borderers of seven killed, 87 wounded and 44 missing. Wounded twice, 'Big Bill' Speakman was awarded the Victoria Cross; four DSOs were also awarded for this action. The battle honour Maryang-San was awarded, and by the time 1 KOSB left Korea in August 1952 two more had been added: Korea 1951-52 and Kowang-San.

Currently based at Dreghorn Barracks, Edinburgh, 1 KOSB is established as a light role infantry battalion combining training, operations and public duties in Scotland. Later in 1999 they move to Cyprus to replace 1st Bn., The Light Infantry as the resident infantry battalion in the Western Sovereign Base Area at Episkopi. (1 LI will themselves take over at Dreghorn - an English regiment in the Scottish capital, in time for the opening of the Scottish Parliament ...)

A side drum emblazoned with some of the battle honours of the regiment, ranging from Namur in 1695 to the Gulf in 1991. KOSB drummers wear trews in the Leslie tartan.

Regimental lineage

Raised 1689 as the Earl of Leven's Regiment by David Leslie, 3rd Earl, and shortly thereafter styled the Edinburgh Regiment. The regiment defended Gibraltar in 1732; and in August 1759 was one of the famous 'Minden' infantry regiments, which distinguished themselves in that battle by not only successfully resisting French cavalry, but advancing to drive them off at bayonet-point. Numbered the 25th of Foot by 1751, they served as marines for a time from 1793, and were present at the naval victory of the Glorious First of June the following year. Retitled 25th (The King's Own Borderers) Regiment in 1805, they took the present style in 1887.

Since Namur 1695 the regiment has been awarded over 130 battle honours, including Martinique 1809, Chitral, Tirah, Paardeburg; Mons, Ypres 1914, 1915, 1917 & 1918, Gallipoli 1915-16, Somme 1916, Langemarck 1917, Passchendaele, Italy 1917-18, Palestine 1917-18; Dunkirk, Burma 1943, Imphal, Arnhem, Reichswald, and Korea 1951-52.

(**Far left**) Dance retains an important place among the traditions of the Scottish regiments, with novice pipers acting as dancers. The pipes shown here are those on which Private Laidlaw played 'Blue Bonnets Over the Border' (now the Regimental March) as he paced up and down on top of the parapet on 25 September 1915 during the battle of Loos, thus inspiring the 7th Bn. to make a fresh attack despite gas and heavy fire. Laidlaw played until he was wounded; he survived, and for this act of heroism he was awarded the Victoria Cross.

(**Left**) Detail of the pipe major's doublet, sash, and kilt in Royal Stewart tartan. From his belt hangs a highly decorated dirk set with semi-precious cairngorms.

(**Opposite, bottom left & right**) Details of the doublet sleeve, plaid, baldric, and pipe banner of the pipe major, 1 KOSB (see also page 64).

(**Right**) A captain wears No.10B Temperate Mess Dress Blue Patrol Order, with white gloves

and regimental cane. This traditional form of dress is worn by some Orderly Officers after 1800 hours. The blue glengarry with diced band bears the KOSB badge - Edinburgh Castle over the Saltire, under the Royal Crest.

(**Below left**) The Regimental Provost Sergeant poses with one of his lance-corporals by a souvenir from the Gulf War, an Iraqi ZPU-4 14.5mm anti-aircraft gun. Among his duties is responsibility for the regimental detention centre.

(**Below right**) An instructor from 1 KOSB at ATR Glencourse talks with the inspecting officer at a passing-out parade. In No.2 Dress, the sergeant wears trews of Leslie tartan, and sports blackcock feathers behind his glengarry badge. He has just been presented with the Accumulative Service Medal, awarded for three years' accumulated operational service spread across a number of tours in regions for which the General Service Medal is awarded.

(Above) The British infantry's pride rests on their continued ability - in an age of mechanization - to march, dig, and shoot. Regular visits to the ranges keep marksmanship standards high. Here men of 1 KOSB train prior to deployment in Northern Ireland. The instructor in the background has the regiment's patch of Leslie tartan on his right shoulder.

(Left) Ever since the start of the Ulster 'Troubles' thirty years ago the accommodation provided for the units serving in the Province has been of a standard of which their political masters should be ashamed. Certainly no terrorist prisoner could have been made to put up with the cramped conditions and lack of privacy normal in the troops' quarters. At least for these soldiers from 1 KOSB the top bunks are vacant, giving a few cubic feet more for stowing their kit.

(Opposite top) In the gathering dusk a 'multiple' from 1 KOSB prepares to leave Crossmaglen (abbreviated as 'XMG') security base to escort supplies to the Baruki Sangar, a mere 50 metres away; on the edge of the town square, it is named after a corporal of The Parachute Regiment killed on that spot. As part of the reduction in tension following the 'peace process' they no longer wear helmets, but still use body armour. Chest webbing is specially issued; it is more convenient when crossing hedges or getting in and out of helicopters.

(Right) On the border in 'bandit country' the helicopter still remains the preferred option for the insertion or extraction of patrols in this predominantly nationalist area. The patrols themselves provide protection for the RUC officers they escort.

THE BLACK WATCH
(Royal Highland Regiment)

In 1997 The Black Watch were honoured to be the last British Army regiment to be stationed in Hong Kong, a demanding duty performed under massive media scrutiny, and to universal acclaim.

The Black Watch is the oldest surviving Highland regiment, being formed in 1739 from independent companies raised to police - 'watch' - the Highlands after the Jacobite rising of 1715. The name (in Gaelic, *Am Freiceadan Dubh*) dates from this period, referring to the dark tartan they wore, in marked contrast to the scarlet coats of the Regiments of Foot.

The regiment had been to the Far East twice before the final Hong Kong posting. In 1944 they had fought behind Japanese lines with the famous Chindit columns; and in 1952 they were shipped to Korea. That July the 1st Battalion had joined the Commonwealth Division as the war stabilized on the 38th Parallel and peace negotiations dragged on at Panmunjon. In November the Chinese mounted a major attack to test the UN's will, on a strategic ridge a few miles from the west coast which British troops called 'The Hook'. On its slopes the British suffered more casualties than on any other battlefield in Korea. Initially repulsed, the Chinese renewed the offensive with a set-piece night attack on 18 November which penetrated A Company's defences. Calling artillery fire down on to their own trenches, the battalion counter-attacked, and in hand-to-hand fighting finally forced the enemy to withdraw. In recognition the Colours proudly show the battle honour The Hook 1952.

With Regimental Headquarters in Balhousie Castle, Perth, the regiment recruits from Perthshire, Angus and Fife. On their return from Hong Kong they moved into Fort George, east of Inverness, originally built after the Jacobite rising of 1745-46 to bring the Highlands under control. An outstanding example of the Georgian artillery fort and designed to accommodate 2,000 troops, it is owned today by Historic Scotland, so The Black Watch have to share it with the public. Currently a light role battalion, they provide the Royal Guard at Balmoral during the Royal Family's annual summer visit.

In mid-2000 The Black Watch will move to Germany as armoured infantry to replace 1 RHF in 7 Armoured Brigade. This is a substantial change in role which will require training in new specialist skills demanded by the Warrior and the other unit AFVs. Some of this training will start prior to the move - e.g. that of drivers and gunners - but most will take place in Germany during a six- to nine-month conversion period. 1 RHF will assist in this, and some of that unit's own specialist staff following a career in armoured infantry will transfer to 1 BW. The new establishment will be over 100 personnel larger, giving 1 BW the challenge of building up their strength by a mixture of recruiting and retention; resources are committed to both these aims. The move is popular with the soldiers: Germany offers more and better opportunities, so it is hoped that individuals will feel less inclination to leave the Army.

(Above) In the final days of Britain's presence in Hong Kong a soldier from The Black Watch looks across the border from the New Territories observation post of Nam Hang to the Chinese town of Shenzen.

(Opposite top) At Headquarters Joint Forces Hong Kong, 1 BW mount a guard in No.2 Shirt Sleeve Order (Review Order). The dark blue bonnet with a red tourie and hackle is special to The Black Watch, and is worn instead of the glengarry of other regiments. The dark blue, green and black tartan, originally known as the 'Government' or 'military' sett, was designed for the formation of the 43rd Regiment in 1739; it may have been based on that favoured by the Campbells, who provided three of the original six companies. (Equally, in a period before true clan tartans, the Campbells may have copied the Government sett.) It was known as 'Black Watch' tartan before the end of the 18th century.

(Opposite bottom left) A guard of The Black Watch perform the evening ceremony at Hong Kong's cenotaph, dwarfed by the skyscrapers of the modern city. They wear the stone-coloured jackets of Scottish pattern No.6 Dress with kilts.

(Opposite bottom right) Rehearsing for another of the endless round of engagements that heralded Britain's departure from Hong Kong, the Pipes & Drums faced heat and humidity. They wear the plain dark blue glengarry with red toorie, and the kilt in Royal Stewart tartan. Note the wristband rank badge of the pipe major. **(Inset)** The pipers' glengarry badge - the Star of the Order of the Thistle with St.Andrew and his Cross, with a Crown above and a Sphinx below (often found in British military symbolism, to honour active service in Egypt).

47

Regimental lineage

1725: Six Independent Companies of Highlanders (mostly volunteers of superior birth) were raised from Campbells, Frasers, Grants and Munros for local security duties. In 1739 these were expanded and formed into the 43rd or Highland Regiment of Foot, commanded by Sir Robert Munro of Foulis; they founded the Highland regiments' reputation for ferocious charges at Fontenoy in 1745. In 1748 the regiment was renumbered the 42nd. In 1758, during nine years' service in North America, they distinguished themselves in battle at Fort Ticonderoga, and were awarded the title The Royal Highland Regiment. It was to be 1861 before 'The Black Watch' was officially added as a suffix, becoming the primary title in 1881.

Since their blooding in the War of the Austrian Succession the regiment have been awarded some 170 battle honours, including Guadaloupe 1759, North America 1763-64, Mysore, Seringapatam, Corunna, Salamanca, Pyrenees, Toulouse, Waterloo; South Africa 1846-47 & 1851-53, Alma, Sevastopol, Lucknow, Ashantee, Tel-el- Kebir, Nile 1884-85; Retreat from Mons, Aisne 1914, Ypres 1914, 1917 & 1918, Loos, Somme 1916 & 1918, Vimy 1917, Hindenburg Line, Macedonia 1915-18, Mesopotamia 1915-17, Meggido, Kut-al-Amara 1917, Jerusalem, Damascus, Baghdad; Dunkirk 1940, Crete, Tobruk 1941, El Alamein, Wadi Akarit East, Sicily 1943, Cassino II, Liri Valley, Rimini Line, Greece 1944-45, Chindits 1944, and Korea 1952-53.

(**Opposite top left**) The Orderly Sergeant holds a Guard Mount rehearsal with the ramparts of Fort George in the background.

(**Opposite top right**) The 1 BW Orderly Sergeant, in No.2 Review Order with red sash, stops to talk to a member of the Regimental Police, who is wearing 'Kilts, Boots and Puttees', the RP's exclusive form of dress. The 'woolly pully' is of the Black Watch regimental pattern.

(**Opposite bottom right**) Dress for Scottish regiments being more elaborate than for their English counterparts, they have a regimental tailors' shop and a slight increment in personnel to man it. This corporal displays his employment badge above his chevrons - the 'B' of a group B tradesman.

(**Right**) A khaki bonnet is worn when working or 'tactical'. The regiment's unique red hackle, worn in place of a badge, was presented to the 42nd Highlanders 'as a mark of gallantry' after the battle of Geldermalsen against the French in the Austrian Netherlands over New Year 1795. On the combat jacket sleeve a patch of Black Watch tartan is worn in the shape of the star badge illustrated on page 47.

(**Below**) These members of 1 BW are kitted out with Tactical Engagement Simulation Equipment: lasers mounted on gun muzzles, and sensors worn on helmet and body harness, simulate realistically the effects of the fire of various weapons, and indicate the resultant casualties. These TESEX exercises held on Salisbury Plain give the most realistic training available short of actual combat, and improve battle skills markedly. While the rifle platoons are armed with the L85A1 and LSW, the 7.62mm GPMG (foreground, on bipod) is held by the MG Platoon of Support Coy. in mechanized and light battalions. (M.Owens/Army HQ Scotland)

(**Right**) HM Queen Elizabeth The Queen Mother, Colonel of the Regiment, presents new Colours to 1 BW at Birkhall, her residence at Balmoral, in 1997. The Colour Party wear regimental No.1 Dress; note that the bonnet is worn without a badge. (M.Owens/ Army HQ Scotland)

(**Right**) A Colour Party from 1 BW parade in No.2 Dress Review Order. Officers' and senior NCOs' kilts are distinguished by the green silk ribbon worn on the front. This dates from the days of the original plaid *(breacan-an-fheilidh)*, a large rectangle of cloth used as both clothing and blanket which preceded the 'little kilt' *(fheilidh beg)*; when wrapped around this was secured with ribbons as an alternative to pins. (M.Owens/ Army HQ Scotland)

THE HIGHLANDERS
(Seaforth, Gordons and Camerons)

The British Army's most recently formed regiment, The Highlanders brought together in September 1994 three great regimental traditions, themselves originating from five old Regiments of Foot. The earliest of their forebears was the 78th (Highland) Foot raised in 1778, later renamed The Seaforth Highlanders. In 1961 it merged with The Queen's Own Cameron Highlanders to form The Queen's Own Highlanders (Seaforth & Cameron). The third element of the 1994 amalgamation was The Gordon Highlanders. These forced mergers are never popular or easy, and the Amalgamation Committee had a hard task to balance the conflicting traditions. The new dress includes elements of all three, including their tartans.

Legend has it that when Lord Huntly raised the 100th (Highland) Regiment of Foot, known as the Gordon Highlanders, in 1794, his mother and sisters helped recruiting by visiting country fairs dressed in regimental uniform and offering all who would enlist a bounty of a guinea taken from their lips with a kiss. The regiment now recruits by more conventional methods, from the Highlands and Grampian region - half of Scotland, including the Hebrides, Orkney and Shetland Islands. The Regimental Headquarters is in Inverness, home of The Queen's Own Highlanders, with an outstation in Aberdeen, that of the Gordons. Now based at Somme Barracks, Catterick, 1 HLDRS is a mechanized battalion equipped with Saxon wheeled APCs, and part of 19 Mechanized Brigade, in turn part of 3 (UK) Division.

The Far East has played a major part in the Highlanders' recent combined history. The 1st Bn., Seaforth Highlanders were shipped east as the Second World War ended, disarming the Japanese in Java. Later, after amalgamating with the 2nd Bn., they spent three years in Malaya on anti-terrorist operations, killing or capturing 100 for the cost of 14 killed and 23 wounded.

Shortly after the 1961 amalgamation with the Camerons to form 1st Bn., The Queen's Own Highlanders (1 QOH) the headquarters and two companies were ordered to Brunei as part of a British force to counter a revolt on 8 December 1962 against the sultan by the Indonesian-supported Brunei People's Party. The oil town of Seria had been seized, but was quickly liberated after A Coy. recaptured Anduki airfield; the battalion occupied the town, releasing 46 European hostages, and the rebellion collapsed by 16 December. As a mark of appreciation for the rescue of their employees Shell endowed the Shell Brunei Welfare Fund, which still helps members of the regiment and their families.

President Sukarno of Indonesia retaliated by launching raids into the adjoining states of Sarawak and Sabah (North Borneo). These joined the fledgling Federation of Malaysia, thus gaining British protection; and three years of almost open warfare followed (euphemistically termed 'the Confrontation'). Later in 1963 1 QOH returned for a nine-month tour, chiefly patrolling the jungle border with Indonesia. 1st Gordons also arrived in the last year of the Confrontation, operating firstly in Sabah and then in Sarawak. Eventually General Suharto seized power in Indonesia and quickly brought the undeclared war to an end, ratifying a peace agreement on 11 August 1966.

The cap badge is that formerly worn by The Queen's Own Highlanders: the stag's head and motto of the Seaforth, and within the antlers a thistle under the crown - the former collar badge of the Camerons. The tartan patch is Cameron of Erracht; also from the Camerons - the last regiment to wear the kilt in action - is the blue hackle adopted as 'compensation' when forced to swap the kilt for battledress in 1940.

Regimental lineage

The Seaforth Highlanders Raised 1778 as the 78th Highland Regiment; 1786, renumbered 72nd; 1823, took the suffix Duke of Albany's Own. A new regiment raised in 1793 as the 78th Highland Regiment soon took the designation Ross-shire Buffs. In 1881 the 72nd and 78th formed the 1st & 2nd Bns., The Seaforth Highlanders.

The Queen's Own Cameron Highlanders Raised 1793 as the 79th Foot, soon taking the designation Cameron Highlanders; in 1873 the prefix 'The Queen's Own' was awarded.

The Gordon Highlanders The 75th Highland Regiment or Abercromby's Highlanders was raised in 1787, taking the designation Stirlingshire Regiment in 1862. The 100th Highland Regiment was raised in 1794, and renumbered 92nd Foot in 1798, taking the designation Gordon Highlanders officially in 1862. In 1881 the 75th and 92nd became the 1st & 2nd Bns., The Gordon Highlanders.

Today's combined regiment are the heirs to some 190 battle honours, including Assaye, Maida, Java, Corunna, Busaco, Fuentes d'Onor, Salamanca, Vittoria, Pyrenees, Toulouse, Waterloo; South Africa 1835, Alma, Delhi, Lucknow, Kabul 1879, Chitral, Tirah, Atbara, Khartoum, Defence of Ladysmith; Mons, Aisne 1914, Ypres 1914, 1915, 1917 & 1918, Somme 1916 & 1918, Arras 1917 & 1918, Cambrai 1917 & 1918, Macedonia 1915-18, Palestine 1918, Vittorio Veneto; St.Valéry-en-Caux, Tobruk 1941, Sidi Barrani, El Alamein, Mareth, Sicily 1943, Anzio, Cassino I, Gothic Line, Reichswald, Rhine, Imphal, Kohima and Mandalay.

(**Opposite top**) No.1 Dress for The Highlanders combines carefully balanced elements from their three predecessors. The badge on the plain glengarry combines those of the Seaforth and Camerons; to balance this the kilt is the Gordon tartan - Government sett with a yellow overstripe. The visible collar badge is the elephant with the 78th Highlanders' battle honour 'Assaye'. The sporran is black with white tassels (for the band this is reversed).

(**Left**) When Her Majesty The Queen is in Scotland Edinburgh's resident Scottish regiments provide guards. Here the officers from the Colour Party of The Highlanders stand in front of Holyrood Palace, her Edinburgh residence, in No.1 Dress. The immediate differences from that of other ranks are the gold embellishments to the doublet, shoulder cords, crimson silk shoulder sash, sword and belt.

(**Above**) The resplendent Pipes and Drums of 1 HLDRS wear the kilt and plaid in Cameron of Erracht tartan, designed by the mother of Alan Cameron of Erracht who founded the 79th Regiment in 1793. The pipes combine the Mackenzie of Seaforth and Gordon tartans; thus all traditions are respected. The sporran is white hair with two black tassels; and a eagle feather adorns the glengarry.

(**Right**) Tucked in the diced hose of a piper is a *skean dhu*, a Highlander's traditional short dirk. The unusual black buttons on the white gaiters were adopted by the Gordons to mark the death of the much-loved Sir John Moore at Corunna in 1809.

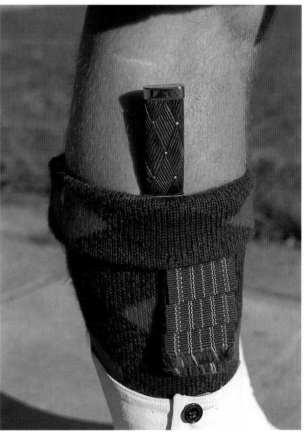

(Left) A young recruit to The Highlanders stands proudly during his passing-out parade at Glencourse. With the introduction of the L85A1 rifle - short, heavy, and with awkward protrusions - ceremonial rifle drill had to be amended to allow the weapon to be moved from shoulder to shoulder to rest the carrying arm.

(Below) As well as being accomplished musicians the members of the Pipes and Drums, such as these from 1 HLDRS, normally double as the MG Platoon of Fire Support Company. Since the switch to 5.62mm calibre for rifle section weapons with the introduction of the L85A1, the 7.62mm General Purpose Machine Gun now provides additional range and weight of fire. Mounted on a tripod in the sustained fire (SF) role it is capable of reaching out to 1,800m (although tracer burns out at 1,100 meters).

(Opposite top) Over the years too many unnecessary casualties have been caused even in the British Army by careless handling of weapons; today loading and unloading drills are rigorously enforced in a loading bay. Two members of the guard from 1 HLDRS load their L85A1s, pointing them into a sand bullet trap under the watchful eye of their Guard Commander. The magazine with the designated number of rounds is fitted on the weapon, but the rifle is not cocked and so no round is chambered.

(Opposite below) An award – winning photograph from 1 HLDRS battalion photographer of Milan being fired on Otterburn ranges. With a range of 1,850m, Milan provides the principal anti-tank capability within infantry battalions; it also has a proven capability against bunkers and machine gun positions. The number of posts in the Anti-tank Platoon varies depending on role, from six in a light role battalion such as 1 HLDRS, up to 42 with 1 RS as part of 24 Airmobile Brigade. (Cpl.B.Nelson/ 1 HLDRS)

THE ARGYLL and SUTHERLAND HIGHLANDERS (Princess Louise's)

Reduced to a single battalion in 1947 after fighting throughout the Second World War in Malaya, North Africa, Italy and North-West Europe, The Argyll and Suntherland Highlanders have since continued to travel the world in the service of the Crown: to Palestine, Hong Kong, Korea, Egypt, Cyprus, Borneo and Southern Arabia.

Landing with the 1st Bn., The Middlesex Regiment as the first British troops into Korea in August 1950, the Argylls went straight into the line on the hard-pressed Pusan Perimeter. Accompanying the US 24th Division in the break-out of 18 September, they made their first battalion attack against a feature called Hill 282. The assault was a success, but casualties mounted from North Korean counter-attacks and shellfire. With ammunition running low and fire support withdrawn, they called for an air strike by USAF Mustangs; but despite recognition panels the Argylls' position was napalmed and machine-gunned in error, killing 17 and wounding another 76. The battalion second-in-command, Major Kenneth Muir, had gone forward to evacuate the wounded; on seeing this tragedy he rallied his men, retook the crest from the enemy, and held it until ordered to withdraw. Mortally wounded, he was awarded a posthumous Victoria Cross. Communist Chinese intervention in November 1950 forced a UN retreat, during which a fierce defensive action earned the Argylls the battle honour Pakchon. When the fighting stabilized along the 38th Parallel the regiment made a welcome return to Hong Kong in April 1951.

One who experienced the ferocity of Korea was Lt.Colin Mitchell, who would command the battalion in Aden in 1967 (see Introduction, pages 3-4). After returning home to public acclaim the Argylls were warned that as the junior regiment they were to disband. A partially successful 'Save the Argylls' campaign kept a single 'Balaklava Company' in being, and a year later a change of government and expansion of forces justified the battalion's restoration to full strength.

With their Regimental Headquarters in the majestic Stirling Castle, 1 A&SH are currently based at Redford Barracks, Edinburgh. Recruits come from Argyll, Dumbartonshire, Renfrewshire, Clackmannanshire and Stirlingshire. Currently established as a light role infantry battalion (see diagram on page 8), they carry out a range of commitments, from public duties to security tours in Northern Ireland.

Regimental lineage

Raised in 1794 as the 98th Argyllshire Highlanders by Duncan Campbell of Lochiel vice the Duke of Argyll; renumbered the 91st Foot in 1798. The regiment served in the Peninsular War and at Waterloo, in the Kaffir Wars in South Africa, and for ten years in India; the prefix 'Princess Louise's' was awarded in 1872, and the 91st fought in the Zulu War of 1879.

At Inverness in 1800 William Wemyss of Wemyss raised the 93rd Highlanders from Sutherland. It served at the Cape of Good Hope 1806-14, in the West Indies and Canada. In the Crimea in October 1854 the 93rd distinguished itself at Balaklava, repelling Russian cavalry attacks while in two-rank line formation - the original 'Thin Red Line' of legend. In 1881 the 91st and 93rd Regiments became the 1st and 2nd Bns., Princess Louise's (Argyll & Sutherland) Highlanders, taking the present designation in 1921.

The regiment has some 160 battle honours, including Vimiera, Corunna, Nive; South Africa 1846-47, 1851, 1852 & 1853, Alma, Balaklava (as the only infantry regiment to receive this honour), Sevastopol, Lucknow, Modder River; Messines 1914, Festubert 1915, Gallipoli 1915-16, Somme 1916 & 1918, Passchendaele, Italy 1917- 18, Palestine 1917-18; Somme 1940, Abyssinia 1941, Crete, Malaya 1941-42, Sidi Barrani, El Alamein, Longstop Hill 1943, Sicily 1943, Cassino II, Caen, Falaise, Argenta Gap, Rhine, and Korea 1950-51.

(Opposite) A sergeant shows some of the Warrent Officers' and Sergeants' Mess silver to a lance-corporal. Both are in mess kit, the lance-corporal wearing trews in the Government or Black Watch tartan. The red jackets are faced with yellow, representing the field of the Scottish Royal Arms. The large Challenge Shield was presented to the mess by the officers of the 93rd Sutherland Highlanders in 1880; it may have been made from silver captured at the relief of Lucknow in 1857 or its final capture the following year - two occasions when the regiment fought with great gallantry.

(Left) A Regimental Police corporal and a colleague from 1 A&SH chat with instructors from their regiment during a parade at the Army Training Regiment, Glencourse. They all wear the blue glengarry with a diced band in red and white only (lacking the blue element of other regiments' dicing); the badge is a wreath of thistles surrounding a circle with the regiment's title, inside which are the interlinked Ls and coronet of Princess Louise, the boar's head crest of the Argylls, and the wild cat badge of the Sutherlands.

(Below left) While the British infantry do not recruit women, each battalion's administration is assisted by attached members of the Adjutant General's Corps, an increasingly computerised function with on-line systems for personnel records, pay, etc. The AGC detachment is normally headed by a female officer and staffed by female clerks; these attached personnel wear a mix of corps and regimental dress. Here an Orderly Sergeant from 1 A&SH, in No.6 Warm Weather Parade Dress, talks with the AGC Detachment Commander; his appointment is indicated by the red sash. Distinctive features of Argylls officers' and senior NCOs' dress are the silk ribbon panel on the kilt front, and the badger's-head sporran.

(Below) The badger's-head sporran is a tradition inherited from the old 93rd. As a protected species badgers are becoming harder to acquire; these sporrans are therefore treasured, and are handed on from generation to generation - some are nearly 200 years old. The one illustrated had previously been worn by a Regimental Sergeant Major. Other ranks wear a plain black hair sporran with six short white tassels, known as the 'Swinging Six'.

(Top) On the ramparts of Stirling Castle, with the monument to William Wallace in the background, Argylls display the variety of barrack and works dress to be seen around the RHQ on any day.

(Above) The only Scottish regiment to have a mascot are the Argylls: 'Cruachan III' is a Shetland pony, named after the war cry of the Clan Campbell. He is looked after by the pony major, a lance-corporal. The sprig of heather on the harness had just been presented to the battalion to mark St.Andrew's Day by the St.Andrew Society, a tradition started in 1991.

(Right) A piper and drummer illustrate the contrasts in their Full Dress. The tartan is the Government sett, but is known in the regiment as Sutherland. While the piper wears the glengarry with blackcock's feather, the drummer has a feather bonnet with white plume. Unlike the rest of the regiment they do not wear the 'Swinging Six' but a grey hair sporran with two black tassels.

(Above) A junior NCO cadre from 1 A&SH discuss section battle drills with their instructor and an exchange officer from the Royal Marines. This exchange recognizes the close link forged in 1942 when 200 Marines from the recently sunk battleships HMS *Repulse* and *Prince of Wales* joined the 2nd Bn. (quickly nicknamed the 'Plymouth Argylls') as it withdrew down the Malayan peninsula towards Singapore Island and eventual Japanese captivity.

(Right) The light infantry battalions are only established with six Milan posts, an indication of their primary operational commitment to Northern Ireland.

THE TERRITORIAL ARMY

At the time of writing (early 1999) the Territorial Army in Scotland - as throughout the United Kingdom - faces another period of turmoil as the effects of the Strategic Defence Review are felt. As announced in 1998, the TA in Scotland stood at 6,900 officers and men - 12% of the UK total. The Scottish regiments included one yeomanry regiment and five infantry battalions:

51 Highland Brigade:
3rd (Volunteer) Bn., The Black Watch
3rd (Volunteer) Bn., The Highlanders
7/8th (Volunteer) Bn., The Argyll and Sutherland Highlanders
52 Lowland Brigade:
The Queen's Own Scottish Yeomanry
The Lowland Volunteers
3rd (Volunteer) Bn., The Royal Highland Fusiliers

The TA infantry battalions had lost their own integral support weapons under the 'Options For Change' reorganization from 1990. They became either 'general reserve', with three rifle companies, or 'fire support', with mortars, machine guns and anti-tank weapons consolidated in two companies - an example is 3 HLDRS.

In addition Scotland could contribute seven other major units: one Royal Artillery, two Royal Engineers, one Royal Signals, one transport and two medical. Sub-units ranged from The Parachute Regiment to The Royal Military Police, from The Special Air Service to four Officer Training Corps.

The TA provides an important link between the Army and civil society, and this connection is particularly strong in Scotland. The local TA Centres provide a physical presence, while the TA soldier as a civilian is active in his or her own community, a constant advertisement for the services. These strong ties have been reinforced by Military Aid to the Civil Community, including assistance when floods hit Perth, Paisley and Elgin or snow causes chaos in Dumfries and Galloway.

Though less than that initially demanded by Land Command, the result of the Strategic Defence Review will still see a significant reduction in the TA presence in Scotland, both in manpower and in 'footprint'. While a higher initial figure was proposed, Army HQ Scotland were forced to accept a 22% cut. The changes will be in place by 1 July 1999.

The Queen's Own Scottish Yeomanry disappears after an all too brief six years. It leaves two squadrons, which become A Sqn.(Ayrshire Yeomanry) and C Sqn.(Fife & Forfar/Scottish Horse) of The Queen's Own Yeomanry, with RHQ in Newcastle. They will, however, retain the grey beret and Scottish Yeomanry badge.

For the infantry things are more serious. With the exception of The Lowland Volunteers the other battalions had only in 1994 re-established their titles as those of the Regular regiments. Previously they had been battalions of The 51st Highland Volunteers or The 52nd Lowland Volunteers. They will now merge to form two battalions, one 'Highland' with headquarters in Perth and one

(Above) The Queen's Own Scottish Yeomanry wear the same grey beret as the SCOTS DG, with a badge of a lion rampant over crossed lances beneath a crown. Historically the Lowlands have a fine tradition of light horse soldiering, from the 16th century irregulars who ranged the Borders down to regiments which crewed Sherman tanks in Normandy.

(Opposite top left) Now only a company in The London Regiment, The London Scottish have an honoured history; they served in the Boer War, and were the first TA soldiers into action in the First World War, at Ypres in 1914. Their distinctive kilt is plain hodden grey - invented by their founder Lord Elcho, Earl of Wemyss, so as not to upset any individual clans.

(Opposite top right) On the east coast training area of Barry Budden, a young member of 3 BW in the assault; note 51 Highland Brigade flash on his left sleeve - the famous 'HD' of the 51st Highland Division in both World Wars.

(Opposite bottom) Indicative of the support given by the TA to the British contingent in Bosnia is this publicity shot of volunteers (including a female chef from the RLC) from SCOTS YEO. They were attached to various units during six months' service with S-FOR; three who were attached to The Light Dragoons so enjoyed it that they agreed to extend their time to two years' Full Time Reserve Service. (M.Owens/ Army HQ Scotland)

'Lowland' centred in Glasgow. How this is to actually work has yet to be announced, but probably the link with the Scottish regiments will be retained at company level, with no attempt to create a new regimental identity. Practical difficulties include the 'lack of critical mass' produced by reducing most locations to platoon size in an attempt to ensure as widely spread a presence as possible. For the Highland battalion another challenge will be the logistics of commanding a unit whose personnel are drawn from an area stretching from Cumbernauld in the south to Lerwick in the Shetlands, a distance of over 300 miles as a seagull flies.

The Engineers face reduction to a single small regiment - although, given their profile as a source of support in civil emergencies, this is being 'negotiated'.

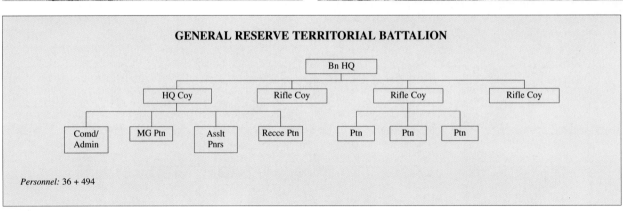

GENERAL RESERVE TERRITORIAL BATTALION

- Bn HQ
  - HQ Coy
    - Comd/Admin
    - MG Ptn
    - Asslt Pnrs
    - Recce Ptn
  - Rifle Coy
  - Rifle Coy
    - Ptn
    - Ptn
    - Ptn
  - Rifle Coy

Personnel: 36 + 494

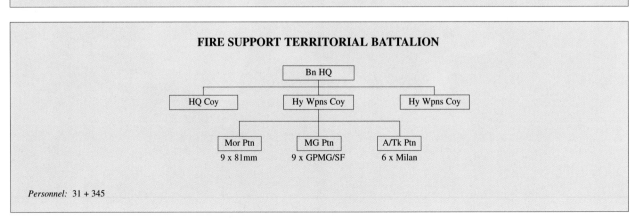

FIRE SUPPORT TERRITORIAL BATTALION

- Bn HQ
  - HQ Coy
  - Hy Wpns Coy
    - Mor Ptn — 9 x 81mm
    - MG Ptn — 9 x GPMG/SF
    - A/Tk Ptn — 6 x Milan
  - Hy Wpns Coy

Personnel: 31 + 345

(**Far left**) The TA have recently played an increasingly important part in bringing Regular units up to strength - a two-way trade, since the TA benefits from the experience their soldiers gain. In Crossmaglen this LSW-armed soldier from the Royal Scots Coy., Lowland Volunteers committed to a one-year 'S'- type engagement with 1 KOSB to join it in Northern Ireland.

(**Left**) Fusiliers from 3 RHF, a Glasgow-based battalion, carry out training at Cultybraggen. Like their Regular parent battalion they wear the TOS with Mackenzie tartan patch and white hackle.

(**Above**) Over the years there has been a gradual increase in the quality of equipment and training available to bring the TA more in line with the Regulars. Here a 'stick' from The Lowland Volunteers double forward to embark on an RAF Puma for a helicopter insertion exercise. (M.Owens/ Army HQ Scotland)

(**Left**) A company commander from 7/8th Argylls listens attentively as his signaller passes a message. His rank slides bear a major's crown above the black title 'A&SH'; below is the regiment's red and white diced flash (repeated on the left side of the helmet cover), above the 51 Highland Brigade patch. (M. Owens/Army HQ Scotland)

(**Overleaf**) The Pipe Major, 1st Bn., KOSB at Dreghorn Barracks, Edinburgh. (M.Owens/Army HQ Scotland)